"THE ART

EDIT

Portrait and Figure Painting

BY

FRANK FOWLER

AUTHOR OF "DRAWING IN CHARCOAL AND CRAYON,"
"OIL PAINTING," ETC., ETC.

WITH THREE COLORED PLATES SHOWING PROGRESSIVE STAGES IN OIL PAINTING

NEW YORK

THE CASSELL PUBLISHING CO.

31 East 17th St (Union Square)

THE MERSHON COMPANY PRESS
RAHWAY, N. J.

CONTENTS.

PART I.

PART II.

PORTRAIT AND FIGURE PAINTING.

PART I.

CHAPTER I.

INTRODUCTORY—A SIMPLE HEAD.

THE fact that the representation of the human figure is generally regarded as the most advanced step in the painter's art seems to invest it with unusual fascination for the beginner. Certainly the number of persons who deliberately choose a course of training that prepares them for painting from life is constantly increasing. These may not all succeed as figure painters, but the advantage of having worked from life will be felt in whatever direction their taste may eventually lead them; so that not only those who contemplate devoting their energies to this particular branch, but anyone who intends to take it up professionally, will do well to begin by entering on the course of study which, while absolutely necessary for portrait and figure painting, will also be found most advantageous in other branches of art. This system is indeed recommended at the best schools abroad, whether the ultimate object be landscape or figure work.

The reason is obvious. The French school—whose influence predominates strongly in America—regards both drawing and construction as essentials to the study of all the graphic arts; and these are perhaps more readily acquired through regular academic training, in the case of the landscape painter, than by confining his practice entirely to outdoor work. From this standpoint, then, these chapters on portrait and figure painting should be of value to all students; and it will be the aim of the writer to make them so. Further, it will be well to insist on the value of this kind of preparation for all who desire to become painters.

The human face presents an area for the study of form and color in the most condensed and most varied combination. The student has here before him tones of elusive subtlety, as well as those of utmost vigor; forms of exquisite outline, and others of rugged strength. The knowledge acquired by a close study of these various qualities, the possibility of becoming acquainted with the resources of the palette under the quiet conditions that indoor work affords, and the attention to outline and modeling which the deliberation of the studio encourages. tend to give one a control of his materials which the distractions of study out of doors will not at first permit.

A glow as subtle as the sky at dawn mantles the young girl's cheek, while for energy of coloring no autumnal tint possesses more vigor than the ruddy flush of health in youth or the bronzed countenance of the traveler in many lands. Catch them on your brush, you who would paint landscape! The portrait painter, pure and simple, has no more need of them than you have yourself. For these, and other reasons which might be given, it is desirable that the student should begin with the study of the head and figure.

It is the intention in this book to be practical, to speak as simply as possible of the technical side of painting; for it is assumed that the reader has already some knowledge of drawing.

The list of colors given below will be found useful in portrait work and will furnish a rich and varied palette:

Silver White.
Yellows { Yellow Ochre, Light Cadmium, Deep Cadmium,
Blues { Cobalt, Permanent Blue, Antwerp Blue.
Reds { Light Red, Vermilion, Rose Madder, Madder Lake, Burnt Sienna.
Greens { Terre Verte, Zinober Green.
Raw Umber, Bone Brown, Ivory Black.

Some portrait painters are constantly making studies of heads in color merely for the facility they thus acquire in overcoming technical difficulties when painting a portrait. Before starting on the actual work of portraiture, therefore, the following suggestions are made for the painting of a simple head:

Place the subject in an effective position for light and shade, and begin by drawing it in with charcoal. Look first for the character of the *mass*. Observe if it be oblong or square, round or oval. This should be the first *fact* to strike you in regard to its drawing; for at present you have nothing to do with features or character—only with *bulk*. When this is determined the features come next in importance. Do they fill the mass of the face, or are they contracted, placed near together, leaving considerable area of cheek, forehead, and chin? Fix this impression well before attempting to define the *forms* of these features. This already will stamp the head with a certain personal character, that the definition of each feature, as you proceed, will only emphasize more strongly.

After drawing with care the eyes, nose, and mouth, in their respective spaces, already indicated, you are ready to begin to paint.

The successful accomplishment of the above is by no means as short and easy a work as would appear from the rapid suggestions given. To get a head in good drawing—that is, all its component parts in the right place—requires much concentration and close observation; when, however, this is done the worker is about ready to lay it in.

In order to retain your drawing, and also to familiarize yourself with the forms of the shadows which you have blocked out in charcoal, go over these with a thin tone of burnt sienna and black diluted with turpentine. As this dries readily, the drawing is secured and ready to receive the color.

Place now, if you have not already done so, some drapery or some tone behind—it may only be the dark corner of the room against which you wish the head to be relieved; but all through your work retain the same effect, and study this object, under all circumstances, in its relation to this background.

Observe now the most obvious effect of color presented by your subject in contrast to the tone that relieves it. State at first the fact of its being fair or dark, ruddy or pale. This is the first impression you will be likely to receive from it, and it is well to proceed with logical sequence. The result will be more potent, more telling—in fact, truer—than it would be if you allowed yourself at the beginning of your work to be attracted by charm of feature or expression. Construct the frame of the building well, and then the ornaments will be an added grace; begin with ornaments and the edifice will be likely to fall. After this first scrutiny, establishing the fact in your mind of the general color aspect of the head against its background, you are ready to paint. We now proceed to actual work.

In the first painting turpentine should be used as a medium, for it leaves the pigment good in texture and dull of surface—an excellent condition for receiving the second and ultimate paintings, when oil is employed.

Commence by rubbing in the background in its proper value and color. This done, the head may be attacked with a full brush, and with as close a reproduction of the effect it presents to your vision, both in general light and shade, as you are capable of making it. Do not look at first for the highest lights nor for the deepest darks. Half close the eyes, and endeavor to resolve this object to the simplest and most direct impression. Mark the tone of the hair in relation to the face and to the tone behind it. Everything should be reduced to the fact of a background with an object, a *spot*, of a certain form and color, in front of it. The contour and proportions will announce that it is a *head*; the subsequent paintings and the definition of the features will tell that it is an *individual*.

To tell this is now your business; and the shape of the forehead, the form of the eyes, the line of the nose, and character of the mouth —each studied with care—will help to make the head a likeness, a personality.

But much besides the mere drawing of individual features contributes to this. The interior modeling, the high lights, half tones, and emphatic darks, the arch of the brow, the energetic or calm lines about the nose and mouth, the squareness or curve of the chin, are all elements in the interpretation of the likeness which must not escape the student. The color of the eyes, irrespective of the pupil, may be now indicated; also the depth of color in the mouth, which varies much with age or physical condition; do not suggest it any stronger in color than it appears under the conditions of the light in which the model is placed. In all that you do try to prove, by the result, that you have referred constantly to nature for the effects recorded. This, more than anything else, will be noted to your credit when you come to submit your work to the criticism of the expert, the painter whose own portrait work has gained him reputation for truth.

In finishing, look for those details which enhance the resemblance and add to the expression. The pupils of the eyes should be touched in with proper emphasis, neither too dark nor too light. Note where the eyelashes cast a shadow, above or at the corner of the eye, and remark that they do not surround the lids with equal force, but are dark only at certain parts, depending on the direction from which the light strikes the head. This is of importance, and the right position of these *accents* will contribute much to the expression and resemblance.

.The character of the nostril is not to be neglected in a portrait any more than are the lines about the mouth; for, as much as the curve of the lips themselves, it demands a faithful reproduction.

The treatment of these finishing touches, as it were, of a face, comes under the head of interior modeling; for the contour may be faultless while the expression, nevertheless, may be unnatural and without character.

Having now some suggestions regarding the method of painting a *head*, it is time for us to consider that more mature phase of life study, the painting of a portrait.

CHAPTER II.

HOW TO PAINT A HEAD.

THE head which is represented by the three colored plates given in this book was done directly from life. In copying it the method employed in its painting may be strictly followed. The study, as will be seen, is given in different stages, which may be called, for convenience, the second, third, and final paintings.

The first stage is not reproduced here. It is achieved by making a careful drawing in charcoal, blocking in the form of the shadows, being sure that the features are correctly placed and firmly defined. As this first state is that in which corrections are most easily made, the drawing-in of the head should be done with much deliberation. The student almost invariably finds that in his haste to go on to the attractions of color he has hurried his preliminary drawing; or at least has begun to paint before the head is in its proper proportions or before the features are in their true position. He finds, perhaps, that one eye is higher than the other in its relation to the line of the nose and mouth, or that the mass of the head is too broad for its length or too long for its width. These are discouraging defects to discover when the whole is laid in with color; but they may be readily corrected while it is still in charcoal.

The head once well drawn, it may be "fixed" by spraying it with "fixative" in the same way as charcoal and crayon drawings are treated. This prepares it for the second stage, as shown in Fig. 1 on the color plate, and such a condition of the work is very essential to its successful termination. It impresses the forms a second time upon the pupil's memory, giving also an agreeable warm undertone to subsequent painting. It consists of a simple flat "wash" of burnt sienna and black, mixed to a certain fluid state by the use of turpentine. In doing this be very particular to preserve strictly the shadow forms as indicated already in charcoal; do not take liberties with them, or else each successive painting will be likely to be still farther removed from the original statement of light and shade; and so new difficulties will be encountered, and demand reconsideration at a more embarrassing point.

Draw the forms of the features very definitely at this time, so as to be thoroughly impressed with their characteristics; for in the third stage, when color is first employed, the *finesse* of these forms is likely to be temporarily obliterated by the movement of the brush, and the preoccupation of the painter to secure breadth of light and shade. I do not insist, in this first laying in of color, that the pupil be over-careful to retain the detail of form in each particular feature after having twice drawn them with attention. It is very essential to mark their position—that is, the space they occupy in the mass of the face; but the vital impression of an object receiving planes of light and shade is in danger of being sacrificed if these incidental spots, eyes, nose, and mouth, are elaborated at this period of the work.

Use plenty of color, and begin working, from Fig. 2 of the plate, by putting in the background. This will provide at once something against which to relieve the head, and it will help you to determine the force of the light and shade on the face in relation to the tone behind. If you were painting the head from life I should advise the same method of procedure—namely, the placing of a particular tone and color as a background, and then painting the head in its relation to it. After painting the background proceed next to lay in the hat and dress in their broad masses of light and shade and color, omitting unnecessary detail until later. Now take up the head, and after observing its effect, as a spot of light against the color which relieves it, put in this light and shade with a brush well filled with pigment, always giving strict attention to the forms of the shadow.

Paint the light and shaded masses as closely as possible the actual color they appear to you; for some of your painting, even in this stage of the work, is likely to be final, if the color is laid on heavily enough.

In your haste to get an effect do not be tempted to paint too thinly. The attempt to secure a certain effect with thin color conduces to timidity in execution, and is a poor preparation for succeeding paintings. Be sure in this first painting to use only turpentine as a medium; it dries rapidly, and makes an excellent ground for the subsequent employment of oil. At this point in the work we only seek the direct impression of the head in its exterior form and color. The eyes are only indicated in their general effect of color—gray in this case—with, as yet, no glint of light in their iris nor intensified dark of pupils. That comes later, and you can readily see that these progressive stages and the simple statement, gained by painting only the most obvious effect produced upon the vision by this human face, result in preparing the portrait for any degree of completion, without loss of vividness or any danger of diminishing the reality of the impression.

We may now consider the third figure of the plate. This is the final result of several later paintings, in which only oil has been employed as a medium. The touches that complete the reality of portraiture are now given; hints that emphasize the likeness should now be looked for and made use of, lurking notes of expression detected and brought out; everything, in fact, that contributes to the personal character of the head should receive the closest scrutiny and be touched in with judgment. Reflected lights, varieties of values, the just proportions of light and shade, the salient notes of color, can be added in this final stage of the work, with little fear of detracting from the truth of the impression; on the contrary, if placed with discrimination these will only enforce the life-likeness of your work.

The same care that insured truth of effect in treating the head should be exercised when painting the dress and hat. The dominant light and dark and all intermediate values must be observed in their relation to the head and to the background. Look with the same concern given to the shadow forms of the hat, for those cast by it upon the head; and note also the relation of the black to the brown of the hair. Put in the dark at the top of the hat, which is not indicated in Plate II., being unessential to that stage of the work. Go on to the dress, finishing in the same way, touching in indications of fold, and giving a sense of modeling by the variety and truthfulness of the lights and darks. Put in the light on the shoulder, which now detaches it from the background, a note it was not imperative to observe before.

Whatever valuable fact reveals itself upon further scrutiny must be made use of in heightening the impression; as, for instance, the high light on the forehead, the touches of light that model the fullness above the eyebrows, the light on the bridge and at the tip of the nose, the touches of light at the corners of the mouth, the accent of dark on the cheek bone and on the chin, as well as a careful study of the half tint which models the jaw and detaches it from the throat—all these are necessary. Look also for the play of light on the hair, the variety

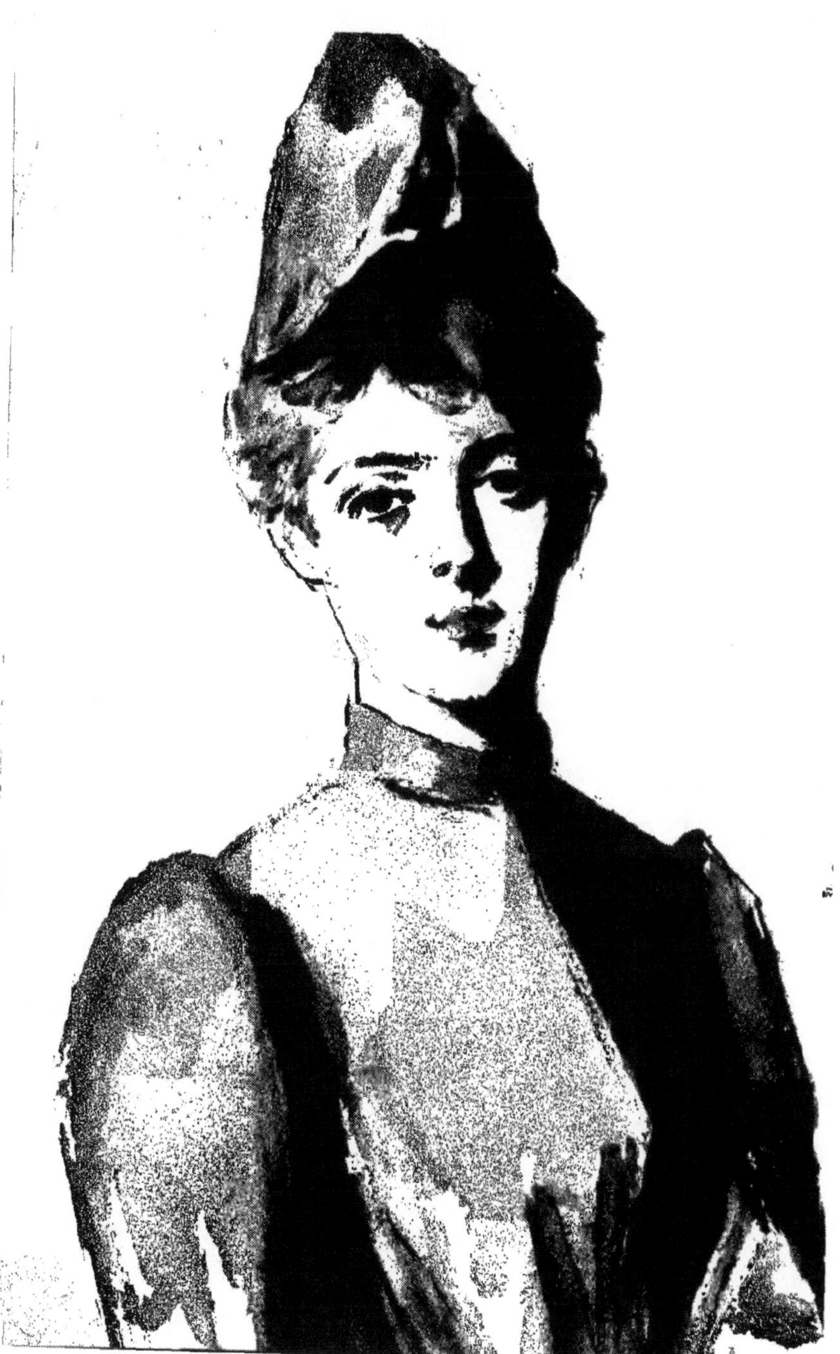

of color that it presents, some notes being brown and others of a grayish or bluish cast. Above all do not neglect the reflected light on the shadowed side of the forehead, for this has much to do with the just construction of the head.

These facts truthfully presented, the head will live in its own atmosphere and possess a vitality that will be sure to impress. This is the mere business of painting, pure and simple, and it is the first business of the pupil to learn to portray—to give the sense of form and projection to a given object in its true color. First learn this, and the initial step in the production of a work of art will have been taken. If the sentiment of art is in the individual he is then equipped to express it ; for he has found his vocabulary, and can talk.

In closing I would recommend those who copy this head in no case to make it smaller than as given here ; on the contrary, if the student feels capable of enlarging it proportionately, the practice will be a good one, and the exercise of covering a larger surface with the brush, sustaining the modeling throughout, will help him in painting from life.

CHAPTER III.

PORTRAIT PAINTING.

THE fact that some of the noblest and most highly esteemed examples that survive to us of the best days of painting are those of portraiture is sufficient demonstration of the dignity of the art itself. To produce a portrait is to do much more than make a mere study of a head. Qualities of composition, balance of light and shade, appropriate accessories, and many other elements of a pictorial and æsthetic nature combine to give dignity to the canvas and mark it as a work of art.

Having now the list of colors and directions regarding the construction and general method of painting a head, let the worker turn his attention to the making of a portrait. It is not now a study merely for the artist's practice that is to be considered, but a person to be painted, whose characteristics are to be interpreted, whose temperament is to be defined. The painter must bring no dormant attribute to light that may diminish the habitual and familiar aspect of the man. This requires mind as well as vision, and it is just here that the portrait painter becomes an artist. He does more than paint—he creates; and to accomplish this successfully requires a penetration deeper than that demanded to present the mere visual impression of the subject. There is much, however, that will aid the painter in producing a work of art in portraiture; and it is to give suggestions to those who wish to fit themselves for the business of portrait painting that the instructions contained in the following pages are written.

THE LIGHT.

This is of prime importance. The usual and safest way of lighting a sitter will be by a high side light; not too high, however, for it is the accustomed, and familiar, that should control a work of portraiture. A light too strong or from an unusual angle, coming from above, for instance, makes two dark caverns of the eye, forms and throws heavy shadows under nose, mouth, and chin. Much of course depends on the character of the subject in regard to the preponderance of shadow or fullness of light that shall be chosen to reveal him. But if the sitter be a woman, fair, delicate, and blond of aspect, choose rather such a disposition of light as shall make the whole head luminous. Avoid in this case any emphasis of shadow more than sufficient to give a proper relief to the forms of the features. Very little shadow will do this, although the difficulties of the painting are somewhat increased.

In the case of a man whose head suggests sinuosities and interesting modeling, choose such an effect of light as will develop this variety of surface without too violent emphasis, guarding always against such an arrangement as will be likely to be foreign to his general aspect. Artists are sometimes so carried away by the æsthetic possibilities of their subject that they forget their business of portraiture, and produce a picture—it may be a picture of much interest, but still an utter failure when regarded as a likeness.

This is a mistake in more ways than one. Nor do not let the worker delude himself that he has done something better than a portrait. To use the means at hand to develop graphically the personality of the sitter is to succeed far beyond the using that same subject as so much graphic material, and with little or no intellectual purpose. Do not, then, be beguiled or lured to failure by the magic of light and shade. Be their master, but let them not master you. The stronger you become in portraiture the more docile and willing you will find these servants, Light and Shade. They will do your bidding, hide blemishes and reveal charms in the sitter. There are painters whose knowledge of the potency of light is so complete and the results of their management of it so satisfactory that they are sometimes reproached as being flatterers, when this agreeable result is largely due to the perfect method of lighting the subject. Do not place the sitter in too strong an effect of shadow—an error often committed by the beginner. Do not, either, divide the face into two equal or nearly equal masses of light and dark. Let the larger area be light.

Study to secure vigor where vigor is demanded, but do not, fearing to be weak in effect, disdain to give delicacy and charm when these are required. Proper lighting will do much to bring out these qualities, and the painter is surrounded with hints that should suggest to him the possibilities of light.

THE BACKGROUND.

After ascertaining the various resources of your studio in regard to lighting the sitter, you may add to the interest of the effect by artificially darkening corners of the room against which you wish the figure relieved. This mode is preferable in many cases to that of employing dark drapery as a background; and for this reason: no matter how dark this material may be—black even—there will be an indication of surface light, which will determine its distance from the object in front. While this is sometimes desirable, when depicting certain characteristic interiors, there are times when the vagueness of atmospheric space gives more pictorial value to the particular subject to be treated. The type of the sitter should largely influence the selection of background. To paint a young girl seated in a heavy high-backed upholstered armchair, the substantial ease of which is significant of comfort to old age, would be an absurdity; and to represent an old gentlemen whose countenance betokens hard contact with the world with a dainty background suggestive of my lady's boudoir would also be a breach of taste.

The *fitting*, always the *fitting*, is to be studied and presented.

In former days, much more frequently than now, it was customary to associate the person painted with his particular occupations or functions by suggesting hints of them in the background. My own good grandmother was handed down to her posterity with cap-strings fluttering in the same breeze that made the schooners scud on the waters of Tappan Zee, which was seen directly over her shoulder; the inevitable red velvet curtain, drawn slightly to one side, disclosed this somewhat stormy aspect of nature, out of compliment to the fact that the subject of the portrait was born on the banks of the Hudson.

So in the case of bank presidents, capitalists, men of large enterprises of whatever kind, the fashion was to use the background as a field for a complimentary allusion, as it were, to the particular prowess of the individual in front. One can recall portraits of hatless gentlemen of eminent respectability, depicted as complacently turning their backs on an outdoor panoramic view of what might be the whole watershed of the Mississippi, with perhaps the Rocky Mountains crowning all, simply because the subject had been a promoter or vice-president of some trans-continental, or less important, railroad.

Pictures of naval officers are in mind where the placid and familiar expression of countenance is in strange contrast to the sea fight hotly waging an eighth of a mile in the distance, behind their backs—the delicate offering of some painter who misapprehended the value and function of a background. It would seem almost needless to say that this is bad art, and that it is to be avoided.

In no instance have the examples quoted shown any coherence between the background and the fact in front—namely, that of an individual portrayed with a view to perpetuating a characteristic likeness under conditions of a normal and natural repose. They are therefore just so far weakened as works of art; hence, no matter how great their technical excellence, they are unacceptable, inasmuch as they fall short of that important element of *taste* without which no work can be entirely successful.

In making these objections to backgrounds of this class the writer would not be misunderstood. The examples mentioned were those where the effects could not be satisfactorily painted with reference to nature; consequently a weak pictorial suggestion was given, and no logic observed in the relation of the figure to the background. While taste forbids this, it does not preclude all indication of a man's occupations or habitual surroundings. On the contrary, when such may be introduced harmoniously in the color scheme, when they tend to emphasize the normal aspect of the man, and are so readily accessible as to be studied in conjunction with the sitter, and directly from nature, they become valuable and legitimate resources, of which it is well to make use.

A geographer with globe or map behind him, a scholar relieved by a corner of his library, a chemist against his retorts, furnish possible and acceptable hints for backgrounds. Still these are only likely to be desirable if the work is intended for some official or professional place. If the portrait is done for the unique purpose of preserving a likeness, the less ornamentations in its arrangement the better. So this question of background will be likely to reduce itself to that of the most fitting. That which will best relieve the head, play most effectively into the contour and add interest to the form, should be selected. Then the matter of color must be considered. When a definite tint is needed to give color contrast, it will be necessary to place the particular hue behind the sitter. Certain complexions demand this, are improved by it, and the portrait gains charm.

Many French painters regard this color scheme as an important factor in portraiture; they make use of a great variety of stuffs of different tints and textures, employing them with actual boldness at times. When some dominant note in the complexion must be modified or enhanced by the background they show great judgment.

The writer remembers a profile portrait of a lady by a famous French painter which was posed against a bright yellow curtain. The complexion was that of high health, a sort of bounding vitality which seemed to pulsate in the cheek, so that under ordinary conditions or surroundings the too florid flesh would perhaps lack refinement. The painter, in daring to relieve it by so strong a yellow, tempered the too vivid coloring to a pearly rose tint which was full of distinction.

It is well to add that such a *tour de force* is only safe in the hands of a master. It will serve, however, to illustrate the considerable part played by the background in the portrayal of the human face, and how judgment and thought, and genius even, marks the selection of an element in portraiture which by some students may be regarded as of little importance.

Another distinguished painter in France makes his backgrounds of an almost unvarying brown tone, laid on with a certain looseness of touch that hints at atmosphere and remoteness behind. He does this with much skill, introducing touches warmer or cooler, as the case may demand, so successfully that this apparently uniform background is never in discord with the color it relieves.

There are, however, objections to its monotony at times; for when some fair girl is to be represented, the severity of the surrounding gloom does not seem in consonance with the subject. Another Frenchman, who was remarkable for the charm of refinement and air of distinction he gave to portraits of women, almost habitually employed a light background of a pearly gray, which might have been a conventional sky in general tone. Into this he touched a variety of lilac, soft brown, and delicate pink notes, so that it harmonized delightfully with the particular coloring of the person painted, adding an atmosphere of softness and femininity to the canvas that was in every way admirable.

A realistic open-air effect employed as a background, unless the sitter be actually posed out of doors, is more than likely to be a failure. And yet there exist portraits where this is apparently attempted, although of course with totally false effect; for a head under those conditions, if truly painted in relation to such a background, could not receive sufficient illumination to define with any exactness the character of the features. Even if a cross light is used the result is unsatisfactory.

An actual outdoor portrait is feasible, but in this light the relation of the flesh to the background is so very subtle that the difficulties of truthful representation are greatly increased. The light being so diffused, the whole visage is illumined with almost equal force; the modeling becomes faint, and it demands the closest scrutiny to develop the various surfaces that give projection and form to the head. Achieving this even, the result as portrayed is likely to be less striking and direct than a likeness painted with indoor effect. From this it will be seen that the safest and most satisfactory conditions for securing backgrounds of permanent and lasting value or interest are to study those representing objects or stuffs receiving the same indoor light as that thrown upon the head and figure of the subject itself. There is another method of managing a background, which was employed in the past more frequently than at present, but which is still made use of with good effect. This is the practice of relieving the dark side of the head by a light tone, and the light side by a dark one. The studio light can be arranged to produce this, so that the tones may be studied actually from nature. When this is done the result is not displeasing, the great danger being that of painting an effect that may appear too obviously prearranged. This need not be so, however, if the balance of light and shade is well considered, and the chiaroscuro made to play its proper part as one element of composition. The light on head and background may be managed in such a way that the sense of relief and projection will be perfectly given, and the head will appear to exist as a living object surrounded by air.

Portraits are sometimes painted where a remote corner of a room, including the perspective of the floor, and some article of furniture, serves as a relief against which the figure is posed. This, too, gives a touch of actuality to the figure or head that is most effective; but it is only valuable as a background when studied in truthful relation to the subject; indeed, every part of a portrait should be so studied.

Plush curtains or damask tapestries, anything almost that goes to make up interior luxury in house furnishing, may be used advantageously for this purpose of setting forth the head and figure of a portrait with added realism or appropriate relief. There is so much to choose from, the selection of which greatly reflects the taste of the artist, that this question of background, it will readily be seen, is no unimportant factor in the production of a portrait.

The quality of tone and color so affects the flesh of the sitter that (as will be seen from the above remarks on the methods of some French painters) the greatest care must be observed in making the tone behind the head thoroughly harmonious with the flesh of the portrait. The whole must be in unity, or otherwise there will be a head painted for itself, and a background painted for itself, making two dissonant facts that will forever clash. Great use can be made of the various hints of color to be found in whatever may be fixed upon as the proper tone to relieve some particular head. If the subject should have black hair, the choice of tone for background with which the purplish blue lights of glossy black hair will harmonize well will influence the eye of the artist as well as the tint of the flesh to be relieved. And in the same way the hair, being so important an element in the general color mass of the head, will largely affect the painter in his choice of color for the background. The *fitting* should always be chosen. Do not paint the rosy charm of infancy with a somber background appropriate to age. Let there be this sense of propriety always between the subject painted and the tone chosen to relieve it. The writer remembers a portrait of a celebrated journalist in Paris, famous also as a duelist, who, although gray with age, was no less feared. The artist in painting this redoubtable writer and fighter did not hesitate to relieve his silvery hair and determined countenance by a background perfectly black. The arrangement was in harmony with the subject; but one would not care to see a dear old lady so severely relieved, when some other and more genial choice would heighten the impression of gentleness in the sitter. Enough has perhaps been said concerning the importance of this part of a portrait to prevent the student from slighting or attempting to paint the background without due consideration.

Do not think as lightly of it as those do who imagine that if they paint the head from life the background will take care of itself. *Nothing* in painting will take care of itself. Intelligence and will must direct everything. There are numberless visual truths of light, shade, and color that play about the contour of a head and figure, which must be observed and painted with a fidelity that can only be secured by study of the actual facts before you. This cannot be done by putting in some imaginary background after the head is finished, and without reference to the contour, to say nothing of its effect on the general tone of the head itself.

Cultivate, then, the habit of observing your subjects in relation to whatever may happen to be behind them. In this way not only truths may be learned, but an original setting to some face be suggested—invaluable in portraiture; for a portrait should not only be a likeness, but a picture. Each canvas of a portrait painter should attest the æsthetic sense of the artist who produced it. Hints that emphasize the type of the sitter may be introduced in the background, or objects which will serve as a sort of antithesis to the character of the face portrayed. Peculiar ornaments, highly wrought, or calm and quiet surfaces, will sometimes come in charming opposition to the cast of head or features represented.

If certain accessories, a bit of architecture, furniture, or anything that hints at space around or on either side of the sitter be projected into the background, the effect is often very happy. A sense of space beyond that circumscribed by the canvas is thus suggested, and in so natural a way as not to appear obviously sought after. It is quite surprising what may be done by art when a true taste directs it. Taste and selection mean so much in portrait painting, they are so intimately connected with every part of the work, that no student or painter can afford to slight anything that exists in the area of the canvas he is at work upon; certainly not that atmosphere, within which a human being is made to stand out as a living personality.

CHAPTER IV.

MODELING.

A HEAD and figure, drawn and colored merely, is not necessarily a portrait in the best sense of portraiture. No great and serious work of this class exists that is not something much more than a *map*, as it were, of the person represented. The coloring may be more or less truthful, the expression may resemble the individual whom it is intended to portray; but the actual *volume* of the head and body, the sense of bulk, one plane leading to another, and so rounding that the beholder is made sensible of another side to this countenance that faces you—all this must be conveyed or the face will be a mere mask, a shell. We all have seen such things, and they are called portraits, but it is almost needless to say that they fail to *portray*.

The human head has first of all a skull, and this frame-work nature has covered with various muscles, cartilages, features, and hair in such manner that the greatest variety is given to its final conformation, although the scaffolding itself—the skull—differs comparatively little in general character in heads of a particular race. Now, it is the business of the painter, in the first place, to hint, as nature does, at this solid construction upon which the ornaments of beauty and character are built.

Light and shade will discover them, color will enhance them, but at all times the sense that the surfaces which charm, or the planes that revolt, have an underlying basis of bone and sinew must be somehow felt. And in every well-conditioned portrait this fact will be apparent—not obviously so, any more than it is in nature, but sufficiently for the purpose of giving the impression of reality and life.

The modeling of a head is of course understood to mean that variation of surface by which the forms acquire projection and relief: this may be rugged or calm, the protuberances may be harsh in character or suave and soft, for the greatest variety of plastic form is to be found in the small area of the human head and countenance.

Light is pitiless, and spares nothing that it falls upon ; but light is beneficent too, and discloses charms as well as blemishes ; so that the whole, the gamut of ugliness and beauty, is played upon according to the character of the forms or modeling that it reveals in the human face. Give, then, this variety as it is disclosed to you ; but in painting a portrait choose that angle of illumination and that aspect of the head which will be most propitious for its interest and charm. Do not, therefore, be as pitiless as light at times can be ; for it can *attract* as well as repel. It is the privilege of the portrait painter to select. In this selection much naturally depends on the type of individual you are to portray. The smooth, calm planes of a young girl's face demand rather a full and quiet light to give that simplicity and directness of effect that is desirable in the representation of forms that possess no bold relief, but which depend for their interest on the placid play of light on surfaces that merge gently from one plane to the other. Such modeling may be kept very simple ; the lightest touch will change the plane. The relief and construction may be attained completely in a very light key of color, so that half tints and shadows used with the greatest reserve will still give all that is necessary of construction and body to the forms interpreted. These same suggestions may be applied with advantage in portraits of infants and children. The eye is so sensitive that it takes in quickly the range of light and dark by which you intend to construct this delicate face ; and in the case of childhood or youth the impression is invariably truer and more entrancing when realized on a high, light key.

There are many instances when the nature of the sitter requires a much more vigorous and dramatic mode of lighting ; when the peculiar surfaces of the head and face call for a marked effect of light and shade. This is for the painter to decide, and students are recommended to place subjects whose faces denote ruggedness and force in such a light that the sinuosities of the modeling and the severity of construction may be fully brought out. This vigorous effect may be obtained by using a high side light and by turning the head somewhat away from it, but exposing the larger area of the face to the direct illumination. Even in a forceful portrait there is such a tendency to exaggerate the strength of the light and shade that I must caution the student against it. Thinking to gain force, he paints the shadows many tones too dark, and frequently forgets that flesh in shadow is not black. Modeling is a much quieter matter in even vigorous work than is generally supposed; and I can recall, now, portraits where in the deepest shadows there is scarcely a hint of black. This intensity is only relative. See to it that your highest light is at concert pitch, so to speak, for the most powerful head may be constructed in vigorous light and shade, and still not be black, nor anything like it.

Look upon a head as an object with protuberances of very slight projection. The nose is the most prominent, and in this sense "an inch on the end of the nose" is a good deal indeed. If so, then the planes of the head most remote from the light are only a few inches farther off than the tip of the nose; and these planes are affected by all sorts of surrounding conditions—reflections from the floor, the furniture, etc. So, naturally, no interstice of the head or face need be as black as a coal hole. The result of any such enforcement of shadow is false, discordant, and out of place.

The beauty of a well-modeled head consists in the reserve with which the painter goes from plane to plane, as naturally as light travels, catching here and losing there, but violently indenting nowhere. There are half tints and shadows existing in some portraits that are so enforced as almost to suggest a wound rather than a simple surface following another near to it. The difference in "value" is not so great as to simulate an indentation or hole.

This is bad modeling, a lack of serious observation. Try to avoid it! Nothing so belittles a work of portraiture as this exaggerated and false insistence on half tints and shadows. It would not be done so often if the painter would train himself to grasp the impression of the head as a whole; to become possessed of the fact that here is an object of varied surface, no one point of which is so far removed from the light that it is not influenced by it. It is *all* illuminated, some parts more, some parts less. Construct it in its simple planes, model it in its varying surfaces, but do this so frankly, so honestly, that the passage from one form to another will be quiet, dignified, simple, and broad.

There is no doubt that the difficulties of modeling are increased when using color; for there is then the additional problem of retaining truth of hue in both lights and darks. This demands a knowledge of the palette that can only be acquired by experience and through many failures. But to succeed finally in doing this is to succeed in much. And this quality of modeling does not apply only to the painting of the head; the form also must be felt beneath the costume, or we will have a human head with the clothes of a manikin.

The writer recently saw a portrait where the head was admirably painted, but it issued from a coat that contained no body. The planes that should have indicated the form within were ignored. No variety was given to the contour, which should have melted into and emerged from the background. Nothing of this was shown; a flat outline of no varying interest terminated the contour of the coat. This was evidently a case where life study only had been followed, and where no attention was given to the study of drapery and accessories.

It is almost unnecessary to say that it is quite as essential to construct and model the *figure* of a portrait as it is the face. If a bust picture—head and shoulders—the forms beneath the drapery must be hinted at, and the play of light revealing shoulder and arms under the material that covers them is always a point of artistic interest to the true painter.

A distinguished French portrait painter has well remarked that a painted head should be so modeled that a sculptor might work from it as satisfactorily as he could from life itself. This statement strongly shows how perfectly the *planes* of the head must be rendered in a portrait. The features may be characteristic, the proportions accurate; but if the prominent and receding planes are not justly observed and given by variations of tone and true emphasis of light and dark the head will not present that *bulk*, lacking which it does not truly exist. The temples are receding planes that form a passage, as it were, to the back of the skull. The face is merely one side of the sphere, yet some portraits are so faulty in this respect of construction that they appear like a section of a head, giving only the *mask*, without even a suggestion that there is a *back* to the head.

The proper management of the *contour* will greatly aid in giving this effect of turning, to the other side. Look for these indications closely. They will be found in the play of light and shade on the top and sides of the head, and just as surely as that there is no doubt in your mind that the head is spherical which you look at in life, so surely should your portrayal of it impress the beholder by its rotundity when painted.

The truthful relation of the background to the varying values of the object in front as they come in contact with it is another way of expressing what is meant.

Of course the interior modeling, being more remote from the background, is more easily compared with those "values" existing closer to the contour and in immediate proximity to the background. If, however, these latter tones are truthful those painted in just relation to them will not be false.

It is in the *construction* of a head that its large and general characteristics lie. The proof of this is in the fact that a portrait strong in this respect may be recognized without the close definition of a single feature. How often do we recognize friends at a distance too great to discern their features! The broad planes of the head are, however, perceptible, and by these we know them.

Much, then, is achieved in the production of a likeness if the student has succeeded in satisfactorily constructing and establishing the planes of the head he is to paint. The interior likeness, the expression, which is more intimate, will logically succeed this strong, broad preparation. And when we come to discuss that topic of portraiture it will be seen how naturally it will follow in the wake of these general instructions on the value and necessity of good construction.

It will be an exceedingly good practice for the student, before undertaking the more difficult task of modeling a head in color from life, to place himself before some good cast and endeavor in painting it to employ the hints here given for the observance of the planes of the head. This exercise will familiarize him with the use of the brush and the manipulation of the pigment, for it will be necessary to get the color of the cast. This will not be found to consist entirely of black and white, and although much simpler than that of flesh, will still demand a fair color sense to secure it. With these frank tones the plane may be more readily seized, the half tints, high lights, and deepest darks can be studied with less excitement, than when encountering these same problems complicated by the varied color and the agitation which is more or less incident to life study.

Portrait painting is such a serious art, its demands are so exacting, the perception demanded for its successful exercise is so keen, and everything about it must be so eternally right, that on the threshold, when preparing the foundation, in a way, on which is built a human

personality, it does not seem out of place to insist strongly on this groundwork.

Lay it solidly. In the first painting use a palette loaded with color, and as a medium nothing is likely to serve you better as a preparation than *turpentine* only. Fill your brush with pigment and paint the shadows with as full a brush as you do the lights. If they are in true relation to the background and to the lights and half tints of the head there will be no danger of their becoming opaque by this method. After allowing this first painting to dry thoroughly you may scrape the canvas somewhat before the next painting, and in all subsequent work upon it use *oil* if any medium is required.

The first painting is a critical one for the success of the picture, for it is in this first attack that you are to establish boldly and truthfully the planes of the head ; hence it is invaluable to have done this with a full brush. While the impression is new and fresh these "values" are likely to be truer and more vital than later, and it happens frequently that some of this first painting is left as the final work of the portrait.

CHAPTER V.

COLOR.

WE have now come to one of the most important factors in portraiture—color. It is perhaps the subtlest element, for it is full of mystery. The hand of one painter may mix pigments that will vibrate and glow, while under the hand of another the same tints will appear to languish and die.

This knowledge of the resources of the palette, this acquaintance with the possible range of the pigments employed, can be acquired only by assiduous experiment. When you are master of this keyboard of hues you may then strike harmonies; but remember that each individual you paint is set to a different key, so to speak; for if you forget this your color will become conventional and mannered. This will not happen, however, if you cultivate that habit of observation which no true painter is without. The charm of nature is its variety—the joy of the artist is in discovery. To a sincere painter nothing is arbitrary. Nominally lips are *red.* Are they red in every person he sets about to paint? Are they not pink, purple, gray almost, and colorless quite, according to the health and habit of the individual he is studying? Observe this, then, and reproduce it truly.

Before giving suggestions regarding the manipulation of pigment it would be well to insist on the importance of close observation. In this way you may become impressed by the dominant and characteristic color aspect of the sitter. Let this fully possess you and you will not be tempted to represent it by an arbitrary or stereotyped scheme of flesh tint. Flesh varies in color as greatly as does individual expression. The dissimilarity may perhaps be more subtle and not so readily distinguished, but the complexion or coloring of no two persons is exactly identical; and the painter who attempts to portray different subjects with a palette pitched in one and the same key of color is likely to be either obtuse or insincere.

The pallid, the ruddy, the high liver, the temperate, the athletic, and he of merely good digestion pass before the vision of the portrait painter, each possessing some peculiar color note that life and habit bestow; each different, all interesting. The sedentary, the active, those of feeble vitality and of bounding health, must be made to live on canvas in the possession of their normal bodily conditions; no more, no less. One often hears portraits criticised as being too florid or too pale for the particular person they are intended to represent. Such strictures are sometimes just, and the artist has in that case failed in catching the salient note of color that characterizes his subject. This sometimes results from starting wrong—on too colorless or too ruddy a key. Try, then, to begin well. Look long and earnestly at your model. The nominal fact of the complexion will impress itself on your mind as fair or dark, florid or pale. This will be the first direct impression. After this whatever variation health or habit suggest will be observed; for in time the scrutiny of the painter will become as keen as that of the physician, who discerns a wholesome or impaired vitality from the external aspect of a man. The painter may go even farther than the physician in discernment, for, as we shall see later in considering the subject of "expression in portraiture," his perception should enable him to discover the *spiritual* attributes of his subject.

Let us now, however, investigate this question of color as completely as may be. It is full of difficulties, full of pitfalls. Much has to be sacrificed to gain it, and unless great care is taken, drawing is completely lost in the effort to paint freely. To confine one's self closely to the line prevents that freedom of touch which has in itself something of freshness and luminosity; therefore it is most essential to have a thoroughly correct drawing to begin with, and such a knowledge of the form and position of the features that you need not be overanxious to retain their outline through all the stages of the work. At any moment, then, when the right tone is found on the palette, the features may be touched in with a turn of the brush, and in their truthful surface value hold their proper place in the modeling of the face.

If this confident method of drawing is not acquired the painting is likely to be labored, and under such conditions pure, fresh color is practically impossible. The mixing of the actual pigment is a matter of much delicacy; for if the colors are worked much with palette knife or brush before applying them to the canvas they have already lost a great deal of the vibrating, luminous quality. Try to drag the brush lightly across the pigments you are combining to make the required tone, but mix them so loosely that fibers or streaks of the different colors remain in parts almost pure. The hue sought for will be made by these component parts, but it is not at all necessary that they should be ground, crushed, or worked into each other in order to produce this hue. On the contrary, you defeat the end you aim at by thus mixing them, for you will produce a tone that will not stand for the hue you sought after it is laid on the canvas. It will be "dead color," and it will not hold its legitimate place as a surface tint in the head you are painting. The expressions "tired color," "dead color," are by no means mere figures of speech. A touch of dead color seems to vitiate whatever good color it comes in contact with; while the right or wholesome hue substituted for it will at once establish the unity of the color as a whole. This goes to prove how fatal dead or tired color is to any right or true painting.

It will often happen that after working for some time in a satisfactory vein of color a touch will suddenly be made that seems inoperative. It does not accord with the rest, and acts as a blight, as it were, on the freshness and vitality of what had gone before. Be sure then that you have overworked the pigment, or that you have added an unnecessary tint to the combination that had already proved effective. Very often mere carelessness, or indisposition to replenish the palette with a tint that has run low, will cause one to take the next best at hand, which is just sufficiently out of key to the hue required to disturb every other element of color in an otherwise harmonious whole. Do not let indolence or indifference work this harm. Be on the alert, and sensitive to these particles of pigment that will sometimes creep into your color even without your knowledge, working over from one part of the palette to the other, unnoticed until on the canvas, and in the wrong place.

This question of color is indeed a subtle thing. Even the right hues overmixed are rendered dull and dead by too much working, and may prove entirely ineffective when laid on the canvas. It is mysterious almost, as I have said before, how, given the same material, one person will call forth living, glowing, vibrating, harmonious tones, and another will produce flat, dull, unresonant hues, lifeless and untrue. One would think sometimes that the very life currents of the painter communicated themselves to the tints he makes use of, for they sometimes gain a vivacity that the tube colors alone cannot possess. It is only possible to give hints regarding the management of color, to suggest what methods are harmful, to tell what practice in manipulation is likely to prove undesirable, and what will mitigate some of the difficulties that a student is sure to meet with. The writer of these chapters pretends to do nothing more than this.

Beginners generally lay on the color too thinly, the result being that the tones are more like stains than actual surface tints. It is impossible in this way to secure a sufficient body of color to sustain the tone in its purity. This thin painting sinks in and soon changes its character of color, so that it no longer stands for a plane of a certain hue receiving light—it is dead—because without the requisite body the pigment seems to be inactive, fails to represent the quality of light upon a form. Without a reasonable supply of this actual material, faithful modeling may not be achieved; for the passage from one plane to another cannot be given unless there is pigment enough employed to preclude the possibility of a change that will destroy the integrity of the surfaces. Paint, then, with a full brush, and load the shadows almost as heavily as the lights. Transparency of shadow is not sacrificed by doing this, for transparency comes by depicting the shadow in its truthful relation to the light, and not, as some think, by loading the lights and painting shadows very thinly. In fact, it is doubtful if a perfectly true relation of the one to the other is to be secured in this way—at any rate the resultant facts are in favor of a solid painting throughout.

Do not "starve" your palette. Put out much more tube color than you will be likely to need, for it will serve for the following day, as only a portion of it is mixed with white in the process of "setting the palette."

Of the actual setting of the palette nothing has yet been said; this is the place to mention it. A uniform system of ranging the colors on the palette is desirable, and when found convenient should be adhered to, for in the absorption of actual painting one then knows in what part of the palette certain tones lie, and he takes up his color from those much as the musician touches certain notes on the keyboard, almost without looking. A direct and simple method of arranging the colors, and one which experience has proved convenient and logical, is the following: Begin at the top of the palette, and near the outside edge, by placing the white, and follow this by yellow ochre, light red, vermilion, madder lake, cobalt, raw umber, burnt sienna, and finally ivory black, which at short spaces apart will more than half surround the palette. From each of these pure tube colors mix, using the palette knife, a certain quantity with white, an inner row of tones, always excepting burnt sienna, which it is well to reserve for rich and dark accents. Prepare these "pats" of color with white while looking at the model, and try to attune, so to speak, this scale of tints to the complexion of the subject. If the coloring of the person you are painting be dark and rich, suggest this fact on the palette in the preparation you are now making; for it will greatly facilitate your work if the palette you set give strong hints of the color aspect of the head before you. And furthermore, the nearer this is set to the prevailing tone, the less actual mixing with the brush will be required.

Continuing this subject of color in portraiture, it would be well for the student to realize the fact that the whole range of tones required for painting any portrait is to be found in the row of pigments placed on the outer edge of the palette, as mentioned in a previous chapter.

These, though comparatively few in themselves, are susceptible of an infinite variety of combinations. In the extremes are tones that represent ruddy health and the pallor of death. But between these there is a range of differences so subtle that the very habit of a man's life may be suggested by the just and clearly stated color aspect of the subject portrayed. There is a marked difference in color between a person of sound digestion and one who is dyspeptic; but no such obvious contrast is found between one ordinarily healthy person and another of somewhat similar complexion. It is of these more evasive yet real differences that it is necessary to render strict account.

It is the province of the artist to observe finely and to report truly. Think, then, of the habits of your sitter. If he is a man of the world, or woman either, the results of good living, fine wines, a leisurely existence, and normal digestion will impart a certain wholesome activity to the skin that is in itself of color interest; quite the reverse of the pallid or bilious or irregularly nourished nature of one who perhaps thinks little of the refinements of actual living, or for whom the anxieties of life have left no time nor taste for its physical pleasures.

These facts must all be considered when in the presence of your subject, for you have the problem presented of placing this personality on canvas in its true visual impression; so that if at any point of your work you are in danger of falling into a colorless key, or the reverse, remind yourself of the characteristics of your sitter.

You will then say to yourself, "This coloring does not represent the type before me." For, instead of the tones of the well-nourished *viveur*, you may have fallen into those of a dyspeptic clerk, or, on the other hand, those of a bouncing milkmaid, if the subject happen to be a woman of the world. These are serious mistakes to make. To prove, however, how seldom this view of portrait painting is taken by artists generally—although one must believe that painters of distinction hold this or some view which answers the same purpose—the story is told of a distinguished lawyer who, about sitting for perhaps the twentieth public portrait of himself, this time to a young and rising artist, made the remark: "Well, what color are *you* going to paint me?" He then went on to say he had been painted as many different colors as there had been artists to whom he sat.

It is a fact that a portrait may be a likeness without truth of color, and the chances are that professional painters will fall into mannerisms. They attune their palette to a certain arbitrary key of color, and it is easier to play the same tune on all variety of features. This method will never be productive of great art, nor is it wholesome in any way. It should be the joy of the painter that in his art he is making constantly new discoveries. No two sitters are any more alike in coloring to the sensitive eye than they are in feature. To a high order of mind this is apparent, and the true artist is always alive to this difference. This seems to me to be the only honest, sincere, and progressive way to look at Nature and to reproduce her. For although this question of color is so greatly neglected, it has so great an importance in portraiture that no single topic has seemed to demand quite so extended a treatment. And yet how many modern portraits are painted in which the personal coloring of the sitter is regarded as of no high importance! An artist would not dare to paint a brown-haired person with hair of black, nor a fair-haired one as having brown hair. These distinctions are too broad and obvious, and may be seen by all. But a painter will often make a fair skin much too ruddy, or paint a complexion, perhaps denoting a fine habit of life in the sitter, of a commonplace and stereotyped flesh tone, indicative of nothing that the subject reveals. This is either obtuseness or mannerism, perhaps both, but it is certainly *not distinguished*, and is certainly not to be commended.

Let it be your earnest effort to seek the subtle truths, which are just as real as the more obvious ones. They are of a higher order and will stamp your work with a style that will be personal, and will speak volumes for your sincerity and love for your work. Try to reach the correct tone by the most direct and simple means, remembering that when the right tint is attained any additional color will only cloud it and detract from its purity. Experience will teach how much of one color or another is needed to modify the quality of the tone, whether it be warmer or cooler than the flesh before you. Try to strike a consistent and united tone. Do not be diverted by the charm of the separate bits of color you perceive in the model before you. Look rather for the whole impression, and endeavor to fix this on the canvas. The desire to paint merely pretty color is a pitfall that many are caught in. What is called sweet color is rarely true color, and it is more than likely to be weak. Think of the pervading blood that nourishes the individual. Remember that the head and hands represent the flesh which is generally apparent in a portrait and is just that which is most likely to be exposed to the influence of wind and sun, and consequently the most vigorous part of the whole body in point of coloring.

The strength and depth of color that mark the best work of the old masters is not due, one may assume, to any great superiority in the pigments themselves, but rather to the workmanlike manner with which these colors were manipulated.

Their tones appear mixed with a lightness of hand that never destroys the vitality of the tints by overworking. Then, too, plenty of the pigment is used. It is almost useless to imagine that thin painting will possess any permanent luminosity. There is nothing to sustain it. The canvas will not, for if the color is put on thin it will sink into the grain of the canvas and make merely a dead ground.

It takes courage and a clear head to mix a large amount of a certain tone and to keep it consistent, and, in addition to this, to have at your disposal all the intermediate tones, the shadow tones and the high lights—all these gradations ready at hand and in such sufficient quantity that you may lift a brushful of any of the required tints and lay them in their place on the exact plane of the head where, so to speak, they most perfectly fit. For we are always modeling with our color, and certain tones as they lie on the palette suggest the plane they will sustain, or the passage that intervenes between one plane and another in the countenance before us. These tones are laid on with a full brush of the required color; for however slight the difference in tone between one plane and another, there is the same demand for the right color and plenty of it: no smudging or thin painting will give quite the true effect, and, indeed, it is never so satisfactorily realized as by frank, solid painting. The most delicate shade of difference in a tone will perfect or mar the modeling: a surface will be made to appear round or flat by this difference of a shade. See to it, then, that you thoroughly understand the operation of the color you use. Experiment with it. Find out what gives projection to, and what causes depression of a surface; and believe always that sufficient modeling may be attained without strong contrasts of tone. The calmer and less violent the modeling the larger and more dignified will be the impression of your work. Sharp contrasts belittle the aspect of a head.

Too much half tint and no pervading sense of light seem to contract the forms and diminish the size of the object so treated. The eye naturally takes in the salient facts of the head—its direct color impression, with eyes, nose, and mouth as prominent facts in the slightly modeled surface. The half tint and accidental notes of color are secondary considerations, and should be sacrificed to the main purpose of presenting a vivid and telling impression of the face you are studying. Let this be given as strongly as possible in the personal coloring of the sitter.

Some painters, of reputation even, paint a sort of generic man in point of coloring at, say, the age of forty, or sixty-five, as the case may be; not an individual man, whose complexion at those respective periods of life differs as widely perhaps as do his personal habits and experiences. A conventional scheme of coloring for a particular age of the subject, is wide of the mark, and for the very good and sufficient reasons suggested above; yet mannerisms of this fatal kind are acquired and practiced more often than is generally supposed. One of the most important objects of this book is to urge on the part of those studying art a constant recourse to nature for all that they do. In the matter of color the practice of referring to nature is supremely important, for perhaps no one element in art work becomes so readily deteriorated if not sustained by continual draughts at the fountain-head, as this very one of subtle, elusive color. So much affects it that leaves mere form unchanged. The interest of a portrait lies largely in its color, else black and white only would suffice for the resemblance.

Now if the tone is impersonal, arbitrary, and does not depend on the subject, but on the whim of the painter, the likeness fails as strict portraiture, and unless the artist be a genius is not likely to be interesting as a mere work of art. Many portraits may be full of interest that are not strictly faithful representations of the subject, but they are works of mature painters, and are not to be quoted as examples for the student to follow, whose aim it should be to possess himself of all the natural facts that may be gained by earnest study.

Strive, first of all, to be good workmen; the production of fine art will come later if it is in you. There is a painter of reputation who years ago studied in Munich; he was very earnest, and full of talent also. One day he painted a head that, although not faithful to the model, was the admiration of the school, it seemed so strong in point of color. Highly elated, he put it under his arm and quietly went to the Pinakothek, or National Museum, and hurried to the room in which are hung many canvases by Rubens: once there, this clever student placed his "strong study" on the floor beneath the brilliant paintings of the Flemish master. Greatly to his dismay the color he had imagined so fine in his own work now appeared dull and heavy, and he took it away as fast as he could, much crestfallen, but wiser. This goes to prove that it is only after long acquaintance with Nature that the artist may take liberties with her, and succeed in so doing, and that too, only if he have the genius to abstract new truths from her. With Rubens it was safe; but be sure that even with him success was the result of patient and faithful study.

Some well-known painters in times past employed a variety of processes by which they attained certain results in portraiture. They first began by laying in what was termed "dead color," almost a monotone; this was left to dry hard before the second painting, in which they imitated the flesh tones of the subject. Such an underpainting was supposed to form a sort of basis which tended to sustain the color applied in subsequent paintings and the successive sittings were carried on over this preparation by different stages until the portrait was completed. This method seems neither direct nor very logical; for the absorption of mind demanded to develop the coloring of the various parts often resulted in very charming "bits," but as often detracted from the force of the work as a whole. And as for the argument that the underpainting sustained the colors superposed and added to their brilliancy, it is by no means certain that the "dead color" was any more serviceable in doing this than a solid first painting in color as near as possible to the complexion of the sitter would have done, for this has the additional advantage of giving an actual impression of the face one is depicting with all the vividness of "first sight," before the mind has had time to become diverted by the secondary considerations of intermediate and unnecessary touches of color.

If a portrait is anything, it is probably, first of all, striking; that is, the semblance of a human being projected on the canvas by another who has seen the essentials of a personality, and reported them truly. And for this reason the student is advised to look only for these essentials; to shut his eyes, if need be, to whatever will distract him, or lead him away from this vital fact; otherwise he will diminish his power; for it is natural to think that the right touch of color here or there will help to emphasize the likeness, which seems so elusive. This, however, does not aid, for the character lies in the broad planes of construction, and in the dominant and salient tone of the head *as a whole.* Seek strength before charm. The charm if it is there will come naturally and without effort: the greatest and most powerful works in portraiture are those in which the coloring appears most simple. Indeed, Nature herself teaches us this. Our friends and people we meet are defined mentally to ourselves as dark or fair, ruddy or pale, not necessarily beautiful in coloring, except as the general impression received may be more or less agreeable.

CHAPTER VI.

ACCESSORIES.

THERE is probably no element which enters into the making of a portrait that admits of such great variety, or contributes so much to its pictorial interest as this of the *accessories*. A wide choice is open to the painter in the selection of that which shall be most fitting. Indeed, the individuality of the subject suggests strongly, at times, what shall most appropriately be used as a "setting," so to speak, of a particular personality. The surroundings should be in good taste and harmonious with the general aspect of the person painted. A sort of natural environment should be selected, so that the figure may appear to belong by right to the material objects that relieve it. If these accessories be well chosen, the personal impression of the sitter will be enforced much in the same way and for the same reason that the carefully appointed scenery in a play upon the stage strengthens the local color of the representation, and emphasizes the sense of reality.

In portraiture, where action is usually out of place, the painter may legitimately resort to those many aids that accessories afford. Be sure, however, that these are chosen and made use of with judgment and taste. Of course a likeness, a resemblance, may be established without the assistance of anything beyond a strict adherence to the facts revealed by the face before you. Paint merely these and you may produce a portrait; but portrait painting as a profession requires more than this. The demands of the time, peculiarities of dress, the fashion of the moment, have at all periods taxed the artist's powers in the work of portraiture over and above facial delineation. Rich stuffs, rare porcelains, furniture, interior decoration or ornament, all lend an interest, and, artistically managed, contribute to the æsthetic value of a portrait. Accessories of course should never be employed merely to fill up a canvas. The right thing should be felt to be necessary, and when introduced there it should impart such a sense of fitness that to remove it would be a distinct loss to the picture.

Whatever, therefore, is introduced into the area of the space represented in a portrait, aside from the subject itself, may be regarded as the accessories; and it is needless almost to add that these should always in a well-conditioned portrait contribute to its effectiveness as a whole. The costume itself is a large accessory to a portrait, and artists of position generally insist that the whole question of dress shall be left to their taste. The very young painter may not have this privilege; but he should certainly, by suggestion at least, endeavor to ward off the filial or sentimental feeling on the part of his sitter which would insist on the perpetuation of some monstrosity of jewelry or a violent color of gown. The early and struggling years of the portrait painter are often darkened by the compromises he has to make between his artistic conscience and the material rewards of his profession. Of course, strictly speaking, everything should be left to the painter, and in time, if he is successful, everything is left to him. The beginner is recommended, however, to be as firm as possible in enforcing his right to the selection of the accessories: even to the dress itself, when engaged on a portrait. In this way the painter makes himself entirely responsible for the production, not only as a likeness, but as a work of art.

It is in the choice of accessories, probably, as much as in any other detail or element of the work, that the painter's taste, or lack of it, may be detected. By one unnecessary object introduced, or by a space filled that would have been better unbroken, the artist condemns himself; for to elaborate without meaning is the resource of the weak. Restraint, judgment, and reserve are as impressive in this part of portrait work as in any other, and quite as essential. Many portraits and particularly, perhaps, some of those of modern painters, suffer from an overloading of accessories; the desire to increase the color interest of the picture is probably the cause of this. But by the knowing, the connoisseur, by those whose opinion is of real value to the artist, and through whose judgment the best reputations are built up and sustained—by these, all subterfuges are detected, all unnecessary elaboration set down as worse than valueless. Portraiture should be real. The more real the more forcible. But to resort to the meretricious to secure reality is to go the wrong way, and to defeat your purpose. Each individual seems to suggest to the thoughtful painter a certain atmosphere and environment in which he will move most naturally.

If this is so it will strike one as a mistake to present a rugged, hard, and rough exterior amid too luxurious surroundings, or, on the other hand, to portray a countenance indicative of an easy and gentle habit of life relieved by severe and inharmonious accessories.

The writer recalls a portrait by a famous Frenchman in which a lady dressed in white satin stood beside a gilt chair. As a background the artist had rubbed in a conventional tone of brown and black which he frequently employed in portraits of men. This ungenial relief in conjunction with such delicate materials as white satin and gold called forth a caricature in a comic paper, in which it stated that the unfortunate lady had fled, at an alarm of fire, from her boudoir to the cellar, and in her confusion had only been able to save one gilt chair. Solecisms of this kind, then, are sometimes committed even by the great, for there was certainly a fair criticism in the caricature.

Whatever is used as accessory to a portrait should be merely an accessory and nothing more: beware of overinsistence on things that should be subservient. The mere pleasure of elaborating some interesting object of still life will sometimes lead the painter astray by giving this secondary factor as much prominence as the head itself. The relative importance of such objects must not be lost sight of. Just as much taste is required in their definition as in their selection.

CHAPTER VII.

EXPRESSION.

THE first painter of any great renown, Polygnotus of Athens, was so remarkable for his power of expression that it was said of his Polyxena that "the whole Trojan war lay in her eyelids." Such a statement of the possibilities of art in its early days should not make us despair. It shows, however, what potency there is in expression, and that it is within the means of painting to portray it.

Nothing, perhaps, in the whole field of painting is so fascinating, nothing so evasive; but for the purposes of portraiture there are few qualities more essential. It might almost be said that expression is the distinguishing mark of the highest intellectual achievement in the portrait painter; for form, and to a certain extent color, may be more or less readily learned; but the ability to define character as revealed through expression seems to demand greater powers of analysis and deduction than those required to attain mere technical proficiency.

Babyhood, childhood, youth, middle age, and old age itself are the most obvious and ordinary conditions that call for treatment of expression which shall unmistakably fix the time of life. There is nothing subtle in this—it demands nothing more or less than precision of statement, fidelity to the facts before you. And yet even here many fail. A child is perhaps made to look too old; old age portrayed too young; juvenility becomes staid; dignity of years is rendered frivolous. This is a vital mistake, but one that is sometimes made by painters. If failures like this are possible, in what case, then, will such an artist stand when subtleties that exact the closest scrutiny to detect require interpretation at his hands? Think of the lines that are worn in the face by the conditions and experiences of life, and of how fierce contact with the world indurates the expression, imparting sometimes a force that is admirable or a hardness that repels. Now if the stress of life ennobles or degrades the expression of those who have battled with existence, there are also facial indications that to the observant eye tell no less surely of a life of ease. A certain emptiness of aspect that suggests no mental activity, no force of will, no power of deduction, no latent possibilities of effort, seems to mark the visage of those from whom life claims no task and exacts no struggle. Expressiveness of feature is consequently wanting in such types, although beauty of form and color may exist. Again, care, anxiety, and sorrow sometimes stamp the countenance with gloomy lines. The artist, however, should avoid perpetuating these, for they are often the result of transient conditions; and who would wish to contemplate forever this depressing aspect of the human face?

Gayety, good nature, happiness, serenity, calmness, thoughtfulness, benignity, patience, self-restraint, high-mindedness, and many other qualities that shine through the countenance and give a permanent, an ennobling, interest to the portrait, are expressions that are characteristic of one or another of the individuals who sooner or later come before the artist for delineation. Perhaps no element in portraits generally is so subject to criticism, and it may be justly so, as this very one of expression. It is not so often the tone of the complexion or the color of the hair that one hears criticised as it is that of the characteristic air or mien of the person it represents. Now this air, this look, lies not alone in the features, but in the demeanor and attitude as well. A portrait must have truth of pose as well as facial fidelity, to be thoroughly expressive. The stolid and phlegmatic are as opposed in general carriage to those who are alert and spirited as they are in feature or expression of face. To give a sprightly attitude to an adipose subject would be not only bad taste, but inexpressive. And it would be equally meaningless to ensconce a wiry, nervous, and active person in the comfortable embrace of an armchair, with a listless arrangement of hands and a pervading aspect of inactivity. This naturally suggests how expressive the hands are of the character, occupation, or temperament of the sitter. To a close observer the hands are a large index to the nature of the person they belong to; they so often supplement certain traits that the visage reveals that one might almost as well get another than the subject to pose for the mouth, for instance, as to take a substitute for the hands. And yet it is no uncommon thing for artists, as a matter of convenience, to paint the hands in a portrait from others than those of the sitter. After what has been said this may be regarded as an undesirable practice, to say the least.

This large view of expression in portraiture is held by many of the most famous painters abroad. During the period that the portrait is in progress, these painters are given many opportunities of studying their subject besides the regular "sittings," which represent the actual time passed in producing the work. That the painter may become better acquainted with the peculiar attitudes of his subject, more familiar with the typical "note," so to speak, of the personal aspect of the individual he is painting, he is often invited to dine, to attend receptions, or to join parties at the opera or theater by those for whom the portrait is painted. In this way numberless hints and impressions are doubtless received that influence the arrangement of the composition, and so enforce the whole *expressiveness* of the work that the picture becomes a portrait of a certain personality in its most fitting and characteristic environment. It is this, as well as faithfulness to facial lines, which enhances the sense of actuality in a work of this kind.

Such strong elements of characterization should not be overlooked. The nervous or nerveless manner of holding the head, the apathetic or vivacious way of sitting or standing, are among the qualities which, if stamped upon the portrait, add greatly to the force of its expression. These attributes of the subject should not, however, be overemphasized in either direction. Care must be taken to interpret peculiarities in such just proportion that a living representation of the person shall be the result. A too marked manner or too decided eccentricity of attitude should be guarded against. By mediocre painters idiosyncrasies are often regarded as of prime importance, and the exceptional made too much of, with the thought, perhaps, that in this way the characteristics of the individual portrayed may be enforced. This, too, is a mistake, the natural resort of one whose mastery is not complete; for when it is a question of a permanent production, like that of portraiture, choice and taste are the factors that should be always present, for these are the elements through which it becomes a work of art.

There are often heard criticisms concerning portraits where the expression revealed is termed unfamiliar, sometimes coarse, vulgar, and so far untrue to the character of the subject. The fault may lie in the failure on the part of the painter to give sufficient prominence to the higher side of the nature before him, which side, if the criticisms are just, is the one more commonly apparent to the world. It is just here that the intellectual effort of the artist comes in—it is his province to select, to choose; and a large knowledge of the significance of facial lines will qualify him to accept or reject with judgment.

There are perhaps few greater pleasures for the true portrait painter than to study the faces that pass before him in the course of a day, when his mind is in the mood to observe, and to deduct from the variety of expressions, the sentiments, the passions, the indulgences, the thousand conflicting feelings that reveal themselves to the scrutiny of his cultivated and sensitive eye.

A well-known actress was once being painted during the production by her of a peculiarly harrowing play—one which stirred intimate emotions, and engendered in the heroine a fierce sentiment of revenge. So powerfully did the interpretation of this character affect the mind and physical condition of the actress that she would come to the artist's studio at times much unstrung, and in appearance more than her actual age. The difficulties under the circumstances of securing a faithful portrait, and one that would give the impression of youthfulness and sympathetic charm, were of course greatly increased. But the painter had known her in other moods, and persistently kept in his mind the aspect of his sitter as she appeared under usual and normal conditions, employing the sittings in portraying the form and color, and waiting for moments when the cloud lifted to catch what hints of the familiar and habitual, such moments revealed. The result was a satisfactory likeness, with nothing to suggest the exceptional conditions under which the work was produced. It is this power of abstraction and deduction that gives the painter control of the means by which to secure truthfulness of expression in the large sense of the term.

The artist should always be alert to the unusual in his sitter. Often the subject comes to the studio tired, depressed, moody, or unhappy. These are certainly not the moments to choose for the delineation of the permanent, the habitual, the normal. Things in themselves transient are ordinarily out of place in a portrait, and especially when the temporary relates to so essential a factor as that of expression. If a passing or arrested action, like that of extending the hand, is in questionable taste when perpetuated in portraiture, how much more to be avoided are those peculiarities of expression which have a direct bearing on the likeness when incident to a fleeting mood that barely outlasts the time of sitting! In this fascinating study of expression it will be seen that the artist who is the keenest observer is the one best equipped for the portrayal of the most truthful and agreeable aspect of the person he paints; for the very powers of mind that contribute to the habit of close scrutiny are apt to make the possessor peculiarly sensitive to exaggeration of any kind in delineating the human face. A sense of fitness in the expression to the nature, temperament, and worldly condition of the individual he is studying will restrain his hand when the exceptional and unaccountable in aspect appear transiently, perhaps, but vividly enough to be recorded: the thoughtful artist in such case should stop before fixing forever an attribute upon his subject that in no essential way belongs to a large and generous interpretation.

The painter is, to a certain extent, the guardian of the expression as well as the expositor of the nature before him, and as he faithfully or unfaithfully performs his office of interpreter will the result be lovely or unlovely, noble or mean.

This is no irresponsible task, the painting of a portrait. It is not to reproduce the person superficially, as so much human bric-a-brac, which is sometimes done—graphically correct, if you will; it is much more; for it is the definition of a human character in fair and true proportions, and if nature has treated it fairly the artist should not step in to degrade. The thoughtful, contemplative expression of the scholar, the lines that bespeak a fine habit of life in relative or friend, are precious documents to regard with pride and to show with pleasure, for they preserve "the very manner of the man." What but power of expression can do this? It is the life of the portrait, and the reason almost of its existence.

Is not this a field, then, to stimulate our highest efforts, and does not this quality of expression call for great concentration of thought, and the cultivation of our best powers of observation? Strive to gain this power, for it gives perhaps the most enduring note in portraiture; and comparatively unimportant as this element of expression may appear, it is the mark of greatness to realize it completely in a work.

CHAPTER VIII.

COMPOSITION.

THE part that composition plays in the making of a portrait is perhaps a greater one than may be generally supposed. It is to a large extent the faculty of composing a portrait well that marks it more or less strongly as a work of art: the art of concealing the art and giving to the picture the impression of nature is largely due to the manner in which a work is composed. There are in this connection a few fundamental facts that might be impressed upon the student which, if observed, will be a great help to him. First of all, is the matter of placing a head on the canvas, and this should be decided while drawing it in the charcoal. Care should be taken not to place the head too low—that is, not to leave too much space between the head and the top of the canvas. The effect is generally more satisfactory to the eye, and there is more dignity of impression if this rule be regarded. In a profile view there should be greater space left in front of the head than behind it. The drapery and all accessories must subserve the demands of composition in a well-ordered portrait; but this should not be obviously done, for there are many and unobtrusive ways by which everything pertaining to the work may be made to assist the purpose of the composition.

In large, full-length portraits the lines of the drapery or the materials employed may be utilized to almost any degree in directing the attention to the purpose of the work, which is to represent a human being in a familiar and natural environment. One should beware of repeating lines or spaces if they do not serve a logical purpose: these may be made valuable or the reverse, according to the intelligence with which they are managed, and in portraits, as in all works of art, it is the judgment and taste that they bear witness to which entitles them to be regarded as productions of fine art. An agreeable balance of light and shade may unobtrusively carry the interest to the head, or the lines that an arrangement of the accessories may give will answer the same purpose.

A true painter seems to feel instinctively what is right in a composition; and it is this instinctive power of choice that distinguishes the artist from the mere painter. It is well if possible for the artist to surround himself with materials and objects that may be suggestive of effective composition in portraiture. Much that is ordinary will prove serviceable. The boards of a floor, the lines of a rug, the recesses of a room, are often employed by painters with great effect. The opposition of volume to slenderness, slightness to bulk—whatever will give distinction, style, to the work as a production intended to charm the eye by variation of spaces and diversity of form—all this may be regarded as coming legitimately under the head of composition when resorted to with the purpose of emphasizing the individuality before you.

There are many instances where these resources have been used with the false idea of adding to the merely pictorial interest of the canvas while totally lacking in an intelligent purpose, and, it is needless to say, resulting in failure. The old Dutch masters were successful in this pictorial sense, making their elaborate interiors serve the legitimate purpose of portraiture. They represented burgomasters banqueting or in their council hall, full of vitality, in the exercise of their social or official relations; and these portraits give an emphatic impression of human beings in their most familiar surroundings.

These pictures, whether the portraits are of groups or of single figures, show that the composition only tends to emphasize the individuality, and that it is not made of importance by a desire of being needlessly pictorial. This is intelligent composition, and is what we should all seek. When we achieve it men in overcoats will no longer be painted in front of velvet portières or seated on inappropriate chairs, and ladies in light raiment will cease to disport themselves in close proximity to stormy aspects of nature.

The modern portraitist often gives a picturesqueness to his composition which, besides contributing to the interest of the canvas, adds much to the vividness of the impression. The accessories, including the costume, are the factors mainly employed to accomplish this. The artful way of making use of the lines and ornaments of a dress so as to carry the attention unobtrusively to the head is an accomplishment peculiarly valuable in the composition of a portrait. To do this successfully requires intelligence and taste, and very often qualities of distinction and elegance are gained by the right use of just such means. Many lessons of composition in portraiture may be learned by studying the taste and sense of fitness that controlled the artist in his selection and employment of material which might easily mar as well as make a work of this kind. It is a fact that in portraiture, as in all good art, the evidences of a human intelligence expressing itself in a superior way in the presence of a given problem, are what should be looked for and demanded. Those who have followed these chapters will perhaps be impressed by the fact that the painting of a portrait is something more than the mere reproduction of the physical traits of an individual. To make the person live in his very habit as a man, is to do much more than is usually achieved by painters. And now what has been said will perhaps help the student to feel that this art is serious business, and that it behooves him to pursue his studies in a most earnest spirit. When portraiture is thus faithfully practiced by the artist the public will in time be satisfied with nothing less than the best, and when such a time arrives, merely visual resemblances will no longer be regarded as works of high art. Be sure, however, that it will take great persistence and character to attain this true standard. Sir Joshua Reynolds tells us "those who are resolved to excel must go to their work, willing or unwilling, morning, noon, and night; they will find it to be no play, but very hard labor," and this is the opinion of one who has touched some of the finest notes in the art of portraiture. Someone else has most truly said that "the highest thing that art can do is to set before you the true image of the presence of a noble human being."

The foundation is thus laid of that splendid achievement, the painting of the human figure. Directness and simplicity are the first as well as the last qualities that a work of art should possess, and the method by which these valuable qualities are secured may vary somewhat, but the end sought by individual workers is largely the same where true art is concerned.

PART II.

CHAPTER I.

FIGURE PAINTING.

THE foregoing chapters on portraiture may be regarded as a sort of preparation for this concluding part of the book on the painting of the human figure.

That the study of the figure forms the basis of art instruction in France, whether the intention of the student be eventually to follow marine, landscape, or any other branch of painting, is sufficient proof of its importance and practical value. What has been so effective in France is likely to influence art ideas everywhere; for, from a purely technical standpoint, the supremacy of the French school to-day is, virtually, undisputed.

The instruction given in these chapters will be as practical as the writer can make it, while presupposing always that the worker has a fair knowledge of drawing to begin with. Drawing is so closely allied to painting that they are, indeed, never really separated; but an acquaintance with the general proportions of the figure, a good sense of light and shade, and an intelligent appreciation of modeling should be acquired in black and white; for all this, and much more, will be demanded when pursuing the more complicated problem of color.

One reason why drawing should be fairly mastered preparatory to painting may be stated with a certain force by quoting the pupil who thought it desirable "to have some place to put the paint." It is indeed most essential to have "some place to put the paint"; and that place should be within the limitation of a well-conditioned drawing.

If your drawing has to be sought for again and again with color, good color will be sacrificed in the search; for a beginner is not equal to securing both by this method. The first element in figure painting, then, is that of drawing. If the full-length figure is to be the object of your study it should not be smaller in size than the ordinary "Academy" drawing, which is the height of a sheet of papier Ingres or Michelet.

In painting, however, the larger the size of the study the better is the practice; for the experience gained in modeling large surfaces is a valuable preparation for portrait work, while the skill acquired in painting on a large scale conduces greatly to one's facility in producing smaller work. The practice, on the contrary, of making "life studies" of reduced dimensions becomes an embarrassment when the student finds himself confronted with a subject that demands life-size treatment, or, it may be, of heroic scale. Make, then, whenever feasible, your color studies of the size of life, or nearly so. This may be done by painting parts of the figure from time to time, and not always the full length. Take the head and torso, for instance, which may be made of nearly the full proportions of nature on a much smaller canvas than you at first suppose. This practice is much followed by students in the art schools abroad, and is strongly recommended here.

See to it that your drawing is strongly and simply blocked in its correct relative proportions, no unnecessary time being spent on refinement of line; for it is assumed that the student has already a good knowledge of contour, and, after placing his figure well, that he will be able to define closely the outline when using color. Too close adherence to the contour when first *laying in* the study is likely to detract from the freedom and fullness of touch that is desirable in the early preparation of the work.

After having made this simple drawing in charcoal on the canvas, proceed to make it permanent. To do this take your palette, and, with a little burnt sienna and black, made thin by turpentine, pass over the outline and shadows with an almost equal force of tone. As this dries rapidly, the drawing becomes permanent and ready to receive solid color without danger of obliteration. The broad forms also are thus impressed on the mind by repeating them, as it were; for this second record of the shadow forms should be done with the model before you, when, more than likely, corrections may be made that will materially improve the first drawing. Whatever contributes to intelligent deliberation in the study of a model is of value, and perhaps no factor so retards progress in art work as that of undue haste. Make a habit of looking long and attentively at the model before committing yourself to the not easily corrected medium of color.

From the very beginning, the mind should be kept alive to the fact that there is an impression to be recorded by the means of form and color, and that truth to this is as essential as the elements of proportion, contour, or light and shade. It may be doubted that this sense of the impression of the object before the student is as generally borne in mind as it should be. The preoccupation to achieve the mere drawing of the model is so great that the fact of representing a certain object in its relative effect is very often lost sight of.

That this impression may be as simple and direct as possible some attention to the lighting of the model should be given. For purposes of study a high side light is best, and the subject should be so placed that two-thirds of the figure may be illuminated. The remaining part will of course be in shadow, so that this proportion of light and shade will not only be satisfying to the eye, but when so divided the essentials of the modeling are sufficiently brought out to enforce clearly the impression of the rotundity and projection the body may possess. Mark well the corporeal volume of the subject before you; it has not only length and breadth, but thickness as well. Projections nearest the light are the most highly illuminated; the planes as they recede from the light pass into half tint and shadow.

All this may be noted before putting brush to canvas; in fact, this habit of observing closely is to be cultivated at all times, so that even while setting the palette, which is not yet done, the glance may take in the general effect, and the mind may reflect on the most direct method of securing it.

The list of colors given in a former chapter will be found to be all that are necessary for the work of figure painting. They are few in number, but by their combination a large range of tones may be reached —all, indeed, that the student should burden himself with.

The palette may be set in the following order if for painting flesh only: At the *top* edge, to the right of the thumb-hole, place first your white, and let follow around the palette, in regular order—yellow ochre, light red, vermilion, madder lake, cobalt, raw umber, burnt sienna, bone brown, and ivory black. Just inside of this outer row, mix a pat of each of the pigments with silver white, the quantity to be regulated by the amount of color likely to be needed in the immediate "sitting." The drawing now made and "blocked in" with burnt sienna and black, you are ready to commence the work of the first or preparatory painting. It will now be important to regard with the utmost attention the effect of the model as a *spot* of color in its relation to whatever may serve as a background.

It is the general impression of the figure in front of this relieving tone that should now demand your closest scrutiny, and, in fact, occupy all your thought. Try to divest it of all the accidents, so to speak, of lights and darks, and seek only to reproduce in this preparatory painting the mean effect of light and shade; that is, do not at first be diverted by the most intense darks nor by the highest lights, but let the broader effect of the simple general masses of light and dark be given in their relative quantities as they fall on the figure.

Paint in the background at the same time that you lay in the figure, and be sure that it is in truthful relation to it. These two grand planes of figure and background well established, the work may go on to any degree of completion, in a logical way, if these main facts are preserved. Let each touch be considered in its relation to the background and to the tones immediately surrounding. Do nothing by haphazard. Do not be satisfied by what appears "near enough" to the value sought for. The actual truth of one tone in its relation to another, by a process of mental comparison, is what you must aim to secure.

It is well understood that this is advice given to those who are learning to paint, not to those who, having gone through much the same training, have perhaps evolved a method for themselves. Whatever stimulates faithful observation and truthful representation contributes largely to the successful practice of a student in painting; and the habit of close scrutiny is one to be cultivated by him at all times. Look, therefore, in this preparatory work for the keynote of the color, as well as for the masses of light and shade. Very often this first stage of the work determines final success or failure of your study. It is not to be begun lightly, depending on later paintings to correct faults. This is the point of departure, and if there is a slight breach here it is likely to widen as you go on. Keep yourself faithful to the model before you in the first as in all succeeding sittings. Perhaps one of the most prominent facts to strike you in regard to the color aspect of a model, if you are working from the nude, is that the head and hands are richer in tone than the rest of the body. This comes from their exposure to the sun and air, and must in no sense be disregarded in making your study, but are to be truthfully represented in their relation to the rest of the figure.

If the model be lighted by high side lights the broad plane of light falling on the head and breast leaves the lower portion of the figure in a comparative half tint. This fact should be noted by graduating the tone from the head to the feet of the figure. It is most essential that the effect of the model in its *ensemble* should be seized in this first attack, for in doing this you will go on with a confidence that comes with the feeling that you are logically right. Note carefully the value of the shadows as they come in contact with the tone that relieves them, and in the same way paint in the light side of the figure, always bearing in mind that if both light and shadow are truthful in their relation to the background the general mass of the figure will be a well-established fact.

In this first sitting it will be necessary to preserve only the large constructive lines of the contour. Any closer attention to the outline at present will be likely to interfere with that freedom of touch which is very desirable in the first painting. Do not at this stage of the work endeavor to do more than as above suggested. All secondary considerations—reflected lights, modeling, refinements of line and color—naturally come later. It is a sort of synopsis, a summary of the object before you, that is at first required, and the student must be impressed with this, and force himself to achieve it.

A sculptor does not immediately curve the mouth or volute the ear in beginning his statue. He blocks in these features in their most elementary forms, and little by little approaches the perfection of their modeling through the different stages of subsequent work. The art of painting may go on as logically; and particularly in the case of the student, whatever he does he should do with deliberation, and with the earnest desire to acquire a knowledge of natural laws and of his material that will serve him in all future work. When the work of the first sitting is completed, in which turpentine only has been employed as a medium, the study may be left to dry for two or three days before work upon it is resumed. If, as already directed, the pupil has laid on the pigment heavily it will be necessary to scrape the most prominent inequalities before painting again. This is readily done when the color is dry, and the surface thus gained is a most agreeable one to receive the color, now mixed with oil, when any medium is required.

CHAPTER II.

THE PLANES.

THE figure having been solidly laid in, with turpentine as a medium, it is in a state for additional work and further study; for in this first painting the student was urged to establish the most obvious impression only of the object before him. If he has been successful in doing this he has now placed on canvas a well-planted figure, good in movement and proportions, truthful to the general coloring of the model, and largely massed in light and shade. No features are as yet indicated beyond the form of the eye cavities and the most essential shadows cast by nose, mouth, and chin.

Set the palette generously as before, using oil instead of turpentine when a medium is needed, and then "look"—do not paint, but *look!* Look intelligently. Compare your study at this stage of the work with the model before you, from which, by half closing your eyes, you may eliminate all but the fact so far recorded on canvas—namely, an object of a certain form and color receiving light from a given side or angle—no detailed features discernible, no great variety of modeling, no subtle refinement of outline. If by this comparison your work seems faithful to the impression you receive from the model you may begin the second painting.

This will be but developing what you have already secured, adding to its variety and interest, while at the same time guarding against belittling the impression. You may add many things and still keep simplicity, carry the modeling on to great perfection and still retain breadth; but to do this the most faithful observation is demanded. The eye is so sensitive that it responds to the faintest difference in the variation of light and shade, and it requires the merest shadow of difference to establish a new plane on the surface of a body or any other object. The failure on the part of a beginner to be simple and broad in treatment comes mainly, probably, from too greatly emphasizing these transitions. In his desire to secure projection, modeling, he exaggerates accents either of light or dark, and consequently breaks up into manifold inequalities the calm and quiet surface of a face, a torso, or an arm.

Do not look at a deep accent by itself nor at a high light by itself; to do this is misleading. Try to realize the part such accents play in the whole mass of the figure, and you will then see how comparatively slight they are. Of course there is a salient high light and there is an emphatic accent of dark in every figure or object we look at, but there are very few which are of equal force. After discovering and establishing the highest light and deepest dark the secondary ones must be given with the same simplicity that nature before you suggests.

Having secured the main effects of outline in combination with that light and shade by which the study exists as a human figure, and not as a pillar or a post, you may begin to block in the features in their proportions—the color of the hair as a mass, and the light and shade which give distinctive form to fingers and toes. In doing this, note the increase of color that marks the extremities. More red, and warmer tones generally, may be found at the ends of the fingers, toes, nose, chin, and throughout the ears; and by thus familiarizing yourself with the normal and habitual aspects of the human body the more readily you will seize its usual impression. *Learn what to look for.* Store facts in your mind for future use.

The purpose in painting from nature should not be to reproduce merely the object before you, but in addition to this to glean facts regarding it that may always serve you in future work. There are general traits common to all human figures whose condition is normal, and there are exceptions to these, incident to the temperament, occupation, or habits of individual figures, that must be particularly noted in studying them with a view to painting. We are at the present stage only to concern ourselves, however, with general laws.

Every figure, no matter how exceptional its coloring, exists as a series of planes before the eyes of the student. These planes are a sort of elementary modeling. When well established they give body and substance to the object, and effectually prepare it to receive that closer and finer treatment in which the muscles are defined and by which the figure actually lives as a supple and active possibility; for the planes may be intelligently rendered, and thus far the study may present a corporeal impression; but until the further step in its interpretation is taken, that of articulation and actual modeling, the work will be considered only as in its second state. It is at this stage of planes that we are to carry it on in this chapter.

You have the relative quantities of light and shade indicated—the darks not of the darkest or the lights of the lightest to be found. Therefore the planes at present are resolved to their simplest effect, a large one of light and another of dark. There are besides these two many projecting or retreating surfaces which cause certain parts of the figure to obtrude themselves or to retire.

These are the intermediate planes which give volume, thickness, weight, to the figure, and once well understood, your study is on the highroad to a satisfactory termination. Many professional artists fail in securing this important element in the figures they paint, and although they may show great technical dexterity in brushwork and handling, their figures are vitally defective in the eyes of those who know what is essential to intelligent and great work. Look, then, in this second painting on your study for those intermediate planes that lead from the shadow to the light, or which recede from the light to the dark.

In modeling the torso there will be observed a sort of path of light following the direction of the most projecting surface of the chest and stomach, and continuing with somewhat diminished force down the legs to the feet. The head will naturally receive the strongest light, but because of its darker tone it is not likely to appear as brilliantly lighted as the chest below it. It is assumed that the nude figure is before us, and that it is illumined by a high side light. Place the broad plane of light on the chest, and follow with a closely observant eye its graduation down the surface of the body. Take note of its lessening force as it falls below the most highly lighted portion of the figure, for it plays an important part in the modeling. The area of half tint which comes between the light and dark mass of the figure may next be studied. This correctly placed, the body will begin to assume a certain rotundity of form, which the passage of the light into the half tint and then into shadow has developed. The figure is not yet modeled, but it has a certain large element of form that the further introduction of intermediate passages will tend to perfect, and which a careful definition of the muscles and articulation of the joints will complete.

The figure as an *ensemble* thus closely studied will give a sense of construction, and convey the impression that this body is built upon a scaffolding, so to speak, of bones and sinews. No agreeableness of color, no softness or grace of line, will compensate for the failure to present this fundamental fact of a corporeal existence, possessing weight and thickness, as well as height; and this can only be done by faithfully giving the forms of the light and shadow as they fall on the varying surfaces of the human frame. Regard, then, as most important this study of construction. Each transition demands its own particular tone, that takes its place by the side of the other. In the face, for instance, the forehead naturally projects somewhat, catching a high light, the shape of this light determined by the form of the protruding brow. The brow retreats to the temples—another plane—requiring for its interpretation quite another tone, and also an intermediate one between the temple and the high light. This is a simple illustration of a study of constructive planes. Without placing with care the tones which are to represent these planes, the forehead will lack character. It will not suggest a skull beneath of a particular conformation, and the result will be a sort of rounded block that might be done by a turner, but not a forehead of some one particular individual, and of no other.

When a study lacks character it becomes commonplace; and the commonplace is not a stimulating atmosphere in which to grow. That which is personal, individual, in a figure is not only interesting in itself, but is so because it stands for so much fidelity of vision and appreciation of character on the part of the artist. The more this sense is developed, the finer this vision becomes, the more valuable are the results produced by the worker. Study, then, each model as a something entirely new, and you will be always learning fresh and interesting facts concerning the human form.

Great stress is laid on this matter of observing and rendering the planes of the figure, because no figure deserving the name can well exist without due attention to this important element in its construction, and also because therein lies a large expression of the characteristics of the model before you; not its individuality, but those forms that stand for its general aspect. And this is what we are to seek in the second painting.

What we have done for the head to give it bulk and rotundity we must do for every other portion of the figure downward. Study with care the tones that cause the planes to retreat from the cheek bones to the ear; those that give form to the jaw and chin, so modeling these surfaces that the transition to the throat and neck becomes natural and unforced. Lines in reality do not exist in modeling. The chin and jaw are not outlined against the throat, as some students and even artists apparently seem to think. It is the *passage* from one mass to another that establishes their form, and a projecting chin or a retreating one, a narrow or a square jaw, is interpreted as such by a faithful observance of the play of light and shade on these varying forms if seen in full face.

The tone of the flesh as it comes in contact with the background, preserving always the value of the background which relieves it, must be given with the same truth that is demanded for the realization of the other planes. In fact, you are learning to paint; and as mere painting is a logical performance, and may be learned, you must use all the hints and suggestions that nature and experience can give to accomplish it. To produce a work of art is a more complex matter, and does not concern us at present. Our business just now is to make a good life study. If you learn this thoroughly well, and the spirit of art is in you, it will surely make itself felt.

If you will now let your eye follow the shaded side of the model as it stands detached from the background, you will be able to detect a great variety in the force of the shadow as it sometimes loses itself in the tone of the ground that relieves it, and again becomes almost clear-cut against the same, owing to some prominence of form that catches the light. This variety may be given by studying the actual tone of the flesh as it comes in contact with the background; in reality, as before said, by a faithful observance of the *planes*. The light side of the figure is subject to the same law of varying value against its relieving tone; the gradations, however, being less marked, it is important that the mind and the eye be alert to record the difference.

In all this second painting the worker must not lose sight of the fact that the light as it falls upon the model is concentrated mainly on the head and breast, and by comparison the lower portion of the figure is less strongly illumined. This effect should be frankly marked at this stage of the work and adhered to throughout; for in the preoccupation of mind that is natural in studying the details later on one is apt to paint an arm or a leg for itself, and to forget that as a part of the whole it must be completed in the relative tone that portion bears to the rest of the figure.

If the truthful relation of these parts is well established in the earlier stages of the study, the danger of losing sight of the effect as a whole becomes less when finishing. Accustom the eye to take in the object before it in its *entirety* when making a study. Do not allow yourself to be interested in one part more than in another because of any charm of line or color some portion of the figure may possess for you, if in so doing you are tempted to give it undue importance. By first blocking in your study in its broadest effect of light and shade, and by next faithfully stating its various planes, so that the body assumes bulk and weight, you will be well prepared to go on logically; but be sure that these two first paintings will influence the termination of the study more than you may at first imagine.

A feeble beginning is most undesirable—it is, indeed, no beginning; and until the work is brought into a state of solid and corporeal painting it will never be rightly begun. A sculptor should be able to block in a figure from a well-considered study at this stage of the work; he should find the passages leading from one salient form to the other so firmly indicated that the broad and general sense of the modeling would be strongly enough suggested to be made use of by him in constructing his figure in clay. Think of the early preparation in this light, and you will perhaps better understand what is necessary to realize in your work when commencing a figure. This thoroughness is one of the elements that is so marked in the work of the great men of old; this is what gives virility to the best work to-day.

CHAPTER III.

MODELING AND CONSTRUCTION.

THE fact that the modeling is as important an element in figure painting as it is in sculpture may not hitherto have been sufficiently impressed on the student. It is, however, a fact, and one that should not be lost sight of.

Sculpture is more tangible, it is true. You may pass your hand over the muscles of an arm, and feel the various undulations of form, whether delicate or vigorous. But sight is as sensitive as touch; perhaps, indeed, more acute. The eye rests on painted form, and demands as truthful a delineation of apparent molded surface as that produced by sculpture. These various surfaces, which describe the position of the muscles, tell where they merge one into the other, where fat abounds or bones lie hidden, is known to the painter by the general term of "modeling." In a large way the *planes* are a preparation for this refinement of form. They give the body and substance in the rough, as it were, and when well established the modeling follows naturally. Where the planes express broad passages of light the intermediate tones succeed these and definitely determine the position of the muscles. The student should endeavor to achieve this without undue loss of breadth in the general impression. This may be done by observing carefully the relative force of these intermediate tones—in other words, by studying closely the *values* of these half tones, emphasizing the darkest darks so that they possess their true force, no greater, no less, than that seen in the model. The student is urged always in making a study to try for the utmost truth of statement. In learning to paint you are not supposed to create a work of art, you are learning to use your eyes and handle your material. The production of a work of art is a more complex matter, and at present does not really concern us. The young man at college who would be an author does not learn fiction; he studies the rules of verbal expression, and if possessed of invention he will create later.

These chapters are practical suggestions which may be applied to one's self and taught to others—they at no time profess to teach art, but are believed to contain many useful hints that may be followed safely in both drawing and painting.

Now this subject of modeling is a vital one when the human figure is the object of study. The eye may be a guide to fairly good proportions, a true feeling for color may give reality to the painting of the flesh; but if the interior modeling be defective, if muscles are out of place, and the passages from one plane to another falsely presented, the figure will not exist as a corporeal object—it will be flat, lifeless, and unreal. Look, then, after having blocked in the broad planes, for these varieties of surface, which indicate the superficial forms of a well-constructed human being.

A figure may be well modeled although untrue in color; still at this stage of your work do not neglect, while modeling and constructing, to keep always in mind the color impression of the subject before you. Attention has already been called to the increase of reds in the extremities and in certain parts of the body. The ears, the finger tips, the knees, the cheeks, the lips — all reveal an accession of reds or pink that must be expressed without in any way destroying the sense of *surface* peculiar to the form in which they are found.

In proceeding with the study, already well prepared, lay in the half tones that intervene between broad darks and lights. Study the various forms they take, and the relative force of the darks. These darks might be mentally numbered, according to their intensity, number one standing for the darkest, and each succeeding lighter tone designated as two, three, etc. It is by preserving the just relation of these adjacent tones that the figure will become modeled, the planes of the nose will merge into those of the cheek, and the cheek in turn will round into the throat, the throat into the shoulders and chest, and so on. It is at this stage of work on the figure that perhaps a knowledge of anatomy is most needed.

The numerous forms, suggestive only, are full of meaning when the muscles beneath are known, and the effect on them of the various movements thoroughly understood. Up to this stage we have been modeling only *apparent forms;* but *construction* now comes in for a large share of your attention.

Construction may perhaps be defined as differing from modeling by saying that where modeling expresses the substance or corporeal aspect of the figure construction reveals the salient points which knit the body together as a whole. The points where muscles cleave to the bone, or fold the one over another, disappearing at the contour by the projection of one more prominent, must all be closely observed and recorded truthfully, or your figure will fail to exist as a normal and well-constructed being.

The worker will do well to compare his study from time to time with the plates of some simple treatise on anatomy. By so doing he will be able readily to account for the external lines of his figure, and also familiarize himself with those muscles which give certain results of light and shade in the interior modeling. The vigorous set of the head on the throat, of the neck to the chest, of the splendid rooting of the arms to the shoulders, are all matters of construction over and above the modeling, the mere presentation of the rotundity of these parts. It is this same demand for construction which will confront you throughout the entire figure. The knitting of the legs to the torso, the sturdy sinuosity of the nether limbs, the muscles that strap knee-cap to knee and foot to ankle, are all essential to the representation of a well-conditioned, mobile human being.

When a teacher or student can express these things faithfully because he knows he is right, because he knows they are there, he will be able to do so quietly, calmly, and without that undue emphasis into which a lack of knowledge sometimes betrays the ignorant. To do all simply, with the broad play of light and shade that nature before you suggests, is truly to *construct* your figure. Many fail in this, and it is a failure that proclaims the feeble workman. The student will find that with a keen eye for the essential points in the construction of the figure a strong result may be brought about logically. Building on the foundation of the well-observed *planes* spoken of in the last chapter, these intermediate notes, these accents which describe the projection of the wrist, the protuberance of the elbow, the vanishing out of sight or the merging into prominence of this or another muscle, is but the natural sequence of an intelligent scrutiny founded on a knowledge of these interior forms.

Great stress is laid on the elements under discussion in the painting of the figure, for although many fail in obtaining them, many may succeed by faithful study.

CHAPTER IV.

COLOR.

THE colors at hand as arranged upon your palettes are susceptible to the greatest variety of combination; but, to be practical, the mean, general, underlying tone is all that should at first receive your attention. Is the object before you fair or dark, ruddy or pallid? Look for the relative effect against the background, and endeavor to establish this with a full brush, frankly laid on. Do not try for a quick result by thin and rapid painting, for this is likely to mislead you, as the forms will thus be loosely indicated, and no solid under-painting, which is most desirable, will be attained. Deliberation is to be cultivated, while haste should be eschewed as a presumptuous sin. Only masters have such control of mind and of material that they may state rapidly and well the natural facts before them; and they only do so by virtue of much antecedent work done deliberately and with intelligent application.

These chapters are especially for students.

Look at the model, and strive to divest it of its accidental lights and shadows, all that breaks it into too great variety, for the first stage of your work in color. Avoid highest lights and deepest shadows. Look below and above them—that is to say, lay in the shadows somewhat lighter than they are, the light mass rather lower in tone than it appears. This will give you a reserved tone, upon which, by superposing lighter or darker tones, your figure will assume form and interior modeling. If this main, underlying tone is truthfully presented, the high light will, when placed, represent the apex of a muscle or of a bone, so to speak, and follow naturally and logically in the course of subsequent observation and painting.

In making a study from life try to be as faithful as possible to the color before you. An arbitrary flesh color is no more true in painting flesh than is one arbitrary green in painting trees. No two individuals are identical in color. It is the business of the student to record individual, not merely generic, facts in regard to color. Fidelity in observation is a large part of one's business in studying art, and if the visual senses are not constantly on the alert merely conventional or nominal color will be the result at this stage of your work.

Now a few words concerning the actual manipulation of the pigments. Do not tire your colors by overmixing, but in making your tones use a light touch, for physical force is not necessary. Lightly drag one color over and into the other; so that after producing the tone you are seeking there may be seen separate strands or threads, as it were, of individual hues still unworked, and living in the midst of the tint produced. This method will give a vibration and life to your color that many fail to secure through an unsensitive method of mixing their tones. In setting the palette do not change from day to day the order of arrangement, for the mind should not be disturbed by looking for the position of any color one may need. The regular rotation from white to black, as given in an earlier chapter, will, if habitually used, greatly facilitate the handling of your tones. Your brush will instinctively seek the pigment required, much as the fingers in piano playing touch the right keys without the glance following them. With the model before you, look for the gradation of color from head to feet.

The general tonal effect will be that of an object lighter above than below, and this should be indicated as well as the actual color impression: it has, indeed, much to do with it, for as the parts of the body recede from the light, they will become grayer and less colorful. Bear this in mind, and cultivate a largeness of vision when recording the first color statement in a study from life. Having once secured this by the most direct and truthful means, you may go on with the work in detail.

Look for the color interest of eyes, nose, and mouth. Observe their relative force as *spots* in the mass of the face. Give emphasis only where emphasis is needed, and seek out with the closest attention the variations of accent and of color that these features reveal. There are eyes blue as turquoises, and others like dark gleaming gems, pure in color as some precious stones, but softened withal by lashes and protecting lids. This gives them a color note of additional charm at times, from the very fact of their peculiar setting. Study this. Notice how sometimes the cheek gains a radiance or a pallor from the glint that seems to sparkle in the eye. Certainly the eye at times seems a keynote to the color of the head. The mouth, too, is of much importance. Lips pallid or blood red, or the many tones between, are to be studied as factors in the complexion of the head as a whole. The nostril and round about it will be found to have a slight access of color, and ears often palpitate with lovely pinks and reds.

It is enough, perhaps, to call the attention to these normal effects of color. Many models will vary from them—some more, some less—but the student should be alive to natural facts, for he will then be more likely to present the exceptions when they are found to exist.

In order to obtain a satisfactory color result, the student must avoid "starving" the palette. No tone can be made that will sustain its character of surface quality, representing a given plane of a given color, that is laid on thinly. It will eventually sink into the canvas or into the underlying thin tone, and ultimately develop into a mere stain. Beware of thus staining your canvas. It is not painting; nor will such a practice ever make you a painter. Look at the figure with a comprehensive vision, and try to state to yourself mentally its dominant color scheme. If your tendency is to be cold and gray when you attempt the coloring of a figure before you, guard against this by giving your attention to those parts which you believe, from physical knowledge, are likely to contain the most vivid and elementary color notes. These you will generally find in the lips, ears, nostrils, and cheeks when studying the head; and at the elbows, finger tips, knees, and toes in painting the body. If these color incidents are made too gray the subsequent result will be cold and colorless, lacking all vitality. Cultivate a love for the life-like, growing tints of animate flesh, and your sensitiveness to their charm will in time prevent your being satisfied with less in your work than you know to exist in the model. It is very true that many appreciate these beauties, and only fail to secure them from lack of experience in the mixing of tones. This subject was treated of in a previous chapter.

A light hand and a strong will must go together. The lady who so admired the beautiful coloring of the English painter Turner, asking him with what he mixed his colors, and receiving for reply, "Brains, madam!" was well answered. One of the most delicate points in the painting of the figure is to fix those first facts of color that will set the key and be felt throughout the work in hand. To do this satisfactorily you must have a cool head, complete self-command, and concentration of thought. You should seek to penetrate the very life blood that courses through the veins and dyes the various surfaces of the subject you are painting. Notice how comparatively delicate and pallid certain protected parts of the flesh appear, while others glow with surface color, or show rugged and bronzed by exposure to the sun and weather. This difference should be keenly observed and truthfully recorded. The degree of your fidelity in this respect will be the measure of "brains" you have put into the work. Indeed, after one has become familiar with the handling of the paints and brushes, it is this faithfulness of vision that demands cultivation. Devote yourself to the study, the beauty, of tone. Endeavor to see it in its simplicity. With the knowledge you have already acquired of the resources of the palette, set to work with the pigments at your disposal to represent those half-hidden tints which, in combination, will produce the tone you desire. It can be done. They are there, and "brains" will reveal them.

Always try to obtain the requisite tone by the employment of the fewest colors possible in its composition. If more are used than are really necessary, the purity of the tone and the quality of vibration will be lost. The needless colors will destroy the perfect operation of the essential ones, and will tend to deaden and flatten the tone sought for.

For mere practice one may try to reproduce a certain color effect with the smallest number of pigments possible. If you nearly approach it by using several, try if fewer will do, and in every case be careful to employ the right ones. Some tube colors possess in themselves the quality that may be only attained by a combination of several others. Choose, then, those which will most readily serve the purpose. An increased vitality and freshness will be the reward of this method, provided always that the whole range of your color box is kept sufficiently restricted. There is a great variety of tints manufactured, many of which the writer would not recommend, while he believes that all that are absolutely neccessary for effective work may be found in the list already given in a former chapter, which is very comprehensive, embracing all that are necessary for general use, and it is unadvisable for a student to lay in a stock of numerous colors which are absolutely useless to him and only serve to increase his difficulties.

CHAPTER V.

COMPOSITION.

COMPOSITION in portraiture has been enlarged upon in some previous articles, but there is still to be considered composition in a more extended field—that of figure painting.

This subject is a large one, for it covers almost the whole range of art. All your preparation has doubtless, in your mind's eye, had this end in view. You have probably thought that to compose one or more figures in a picture would be to create—that it would be original work. But let us look at this question of composition a little more closely. To place one or more figures on a canvas is not much of an achievement unless there be a desire at the back of it really to express something. The mere presentation in form and color of a figure or of any number of figures in a given space is not necessarily to produce a composition.

Early art, and even more recent, modern art, had rules which seemed to guide the painters. We hear of the pyramidal, the oblong, and various other terms, denoting different styles of composition—"arrangement" would be the better definition. Now "arrangements" may be skillful, even scholarly, but they can never stand for compositions in the highest sense,

Avoid the commonplace. Before beginning a subject have no other thought than that of presenting it forcibly and directly in all its essential significance. Do not allow petty facts to obtrude themselves, as some weak painters do, for the opportunity they may offer of displaying "clever bits of painting." Compositions are not conceived to show dexterity, thence to excite wonder, but rather with a view to expressing emotion, or to touch the imagination. It is necessary to feel deeply and to report truly: be sure not to emphasize too obviously unimportant accessories. Composition is a form of expression: a subject should not be chosen to exhibit the painter, but to present the idea. A large nature will sacrifice everything that may weaken the force of such expression, while a small nature will smother the idea with an ostentatious cleverness of technique. Such a method offends every law of noble composition: it is rather the sign-manual of vulgar talent than of genius.

Taste and judgment, the expression of a really artistic temperament, mark all works which come truly from within. Those that are produced and carried on from without are likely to be replete with superficialities. The inferior artist prefers rather applause for technical industry than appreciation of powers of mind: indeed, we may simply call him an inferior artist; for if he possessed great powers of mind he would be incapable of "robbing Peter to pay Paul."

One cannot but feel how utterly impossible it would be for an earnest, vehement painter, full of his subject, to give ignoble attention to unnecessary things. The turn of a button, the definition of an ornament, will receive from him no more elaboration than is justly its due in the whole scheme and conception of the work in hand. Fascinating surfaces, felicity of coloring, are only fascinating and felicitous now as they may conduce to the emphasis of the impression he would convey. It is just here in a composition that a man shows his judgment and force of will. A thing charming in itself becomes offensive when out of place: the accompaniments of gayety and pleasure turn sinister when tragedy is the theme. They may be there, but in the hands of a master their lighter features will only contribute in some just proportion to the general aspect of dread the scene portrays. Composition in this sense becomes creation; it emanates from the emotions, from nature—it is not "arrangement," it is life. Take, for example, some stirring scene such as Gérôme might choose to paint—antecedent discussion, high words, blows, crime! Prevalent disorder, in no matter how fair environment, will be visible—the very course the turbulence has taken may be traced. Everything is logical, because intelligence, mental power, directs this graphic presentation. Nothing to weaken, everything to enforce the impression that unloosed passions and actual physical strife within a given area have held temporary sway. Disorder, haste, frail things fractured, and a general confusion where formality reigned before—these are some of the conditions a well-conceived drama of this character is likely to present. In a composition thus carried out you will find that only the fitting, the appropriate, the telling, have been admitted. Gérôme has been greatly admired for his superior drawing and conscientious workmanship: his canvases reveal much more than this—they tell of an intellectual personality behind the brush which can conceive and present a picturesque situation or historical incident in a logical and faithful manner. His compositions are more than schölarly by virtue of his human grasp of both antecedent and subsequent conditions. This is the mental attitude that should characterize one on undertaking a composition. It is not only scholarship but instinct that is needed. A power of choice, which is the possession of the true artist, this should be unerring. In many masters it seems to be.

Nothing should exist in the whole field of the subject depicted, the removal of which would not injure the balance and weaken the force of the presentation; and it may be said with equal truth that no perfect composition may be added to, without suffering a like loss.

In a certain sense, composition is the goal to which all one's efforts in the study of art are directed; drawing and painting without composition would be practically useless, for if one has the persistence to carry life studies to an advanced point of proficiency it must be because he has finally something to say. Not merely for the purpose of telling some trifling story is it likely that all these exhaustive studies have been made: severe and intelligent work, on the contrary, prepares the mind for something higher than trifles. Indeed, I have been struck by the fact that triviality of matter is frequently accompanied by feeble and inadequate technique: robust thought must have forceful expression; and no strong painter who becomes imbued with an idea will be able to express it satisfactorily on the canvas by merely the means of a well-"arranged" tableau. Right feeling revolts against staginess, however clever: judgment, taste, and feeling are essential in making a good composition. If the subject be a portrait, one should decide from the physical characteristics of the person to be represented how the light shall fall in order to give the dominant charm or salient feature of the sitter to advantage. Great mistakes in this regard are sometimes made in portraiture, when that which should be hidden is revealed, and that which should be emphasized made unimportant.

An intelligent balance of light and shade will always secure a characteristic revelation of a personality; while on the artistic disposition of the figure in the area of the canvas, or, in other words, on its composition, rests its claims to be called a work of art. Try to place each particular individual in his habitual surroundings, giving the impression of the person as belonging there and not elsewhere. There are portraits existent showing the sitter distinctly having his portrait painted, and evidently wishing he were anywhere but where he is. This is hardly successful composition, for more reasons than one.

In figure subjects dealing with themes of daily life and peasant toil, the French painter Millet shows a sense of composition that is masterly. Whatever scene he presents, all the conditions of its immediate surroundings are thoroughly felt by him, and the antecedent action leading up to the moment chosen by the artist for his composition is most logically indicated by him. The figures are instinctively in the right place—where the action, incident, or fact is portrayed. No adding to this area nor taking from it may be done without injuring the perfect setting of the scene. There is nothing useless in it, nothing introduced merely to "fill up"—a practice which Millet held in contempt. His compositions are conceived with the utmost fidelity to the character of the incident he would portray. Physical laws are logically respected—a burden is a load under which its bearer totters, weighed down by just so much—not more, not less. It is for the unintelligent to exceed or understate such indications of physical effort. Millet's judgment is always sound. This knowledge, which should be a part of a painter's equipment, is not always employed with this rare judgment. When it is so employed it stands for right feeling, a power of deduction, a sensitiveness to nature's laws that marks its possessor as a man of distinction. Only a strong purpose can strip a graphic scene of unnecessary detail and reveal it in its simplicity. Composition is the presentation of a conception; thus if a thing is poorly conceived the presentation will be feeble. The remark often made that certain "bits" in a picture are very cleverly handled, really condemns the work in the highest sense; for a charmingly turned wrist, an attractive piece of still life, if noted as such in a composition of importance, where these things are mere accessories, suggest that the work as a whole is a failure. An artist well warmed to his subject will give these incidental things the significant touch they demand as contributions to the main interest of the work, but he will not pause to elaborate objects which, if developed out of a just proportion to their importance, would only tend to divert attention from the purpose in hand, which is to present a theme forcibly. It is trivial for a painter to insist on the burnish of silver, the flash of a diamond, or on any other unimportant object that exists in the area of the scene he is picturing, merely because he is particularly skillful in the portrayal of such accessories. The fact that he does so convicts him of superficiality, and a lack of taste, judgment, and feeling.

We have now been over a large field in the practical study of painting. Portrait and figure painting have been seriously discussed, and have received a large share of attention. The writer asks the student to bear in mind that he has at no time desired to be didactic, but has only been moved by the wish to advance suggestions that will tend to simplify and give directness to the study of painting. It is his earnest hope that such hints may be made fruitful of much good. If what has been written on these subjects tends to stimulate a desire in the reader to devote himself more closely to the study of nature in its relation to art, the purpose of these chapters will have been accomplished.

THE END.

CPSIA information can be obtained
at www.ICGtesting.com
Printed in the USA
LVHW051738250623
750731LV00011B/1336